Equity Investments and Fixed Income: CFA Level 1 Guide

Azhar ul Haque Sario

Copyright

First Printing, 2025

Azhar.sario@hotmail.co.uk

ORCID: https://orcid.org/0009-0004-8629-830X
LinkedIn: https://www.linkedin.com/in/azharulhaquesario/

Disclaimer: This book is free from AI use. The cover was designed in Canva.

Contents

Subject 1: Equity Investments

Market Organization and Structure

1. The Symphony of the System: What Finance Really Does

Imagine an economy not as a machine, but as a living, breathing organism. If so, the financial system is its circulatory system. It's the intricate network of veins and arteries that carries the lifeblood—money—from where it pools to where it's needed most. Its job isn't just to move money around; it's to breathe life into dreams, ambitions, and innovations.

At its heart, its most profound function is to channel dreams into reality. Think of all the savings tucked away in accounts, like water collected in a vast reservoir. On the other side of the country, an entrepreneur has a brilliant idea for a new kind of energy, a family wants to build their first home, a student needs tuition to become a doctor. The financial system is the brilliant network of aqueducts and canals that connects that quiet reservoir of savings to these thirsty, fertile fields of opportunity. Without it, savings would sit stagnant, and great ideas would wither on the vine.

Next, it acts as a collective brain for discovering value. Picture a bustling global marketplace, not of spices and silks, but of ideas and futures. Every time someone buys a share of a company or a barrel of oil, they're casting a vote with their money, saying, "I believe in this." The price that emerges from this chaotic, constant voting is a kind of public wisdom. It's a signal, shining brightly for all to see, that tells us which ventures society values and where our collective energy should flow. This "price discovery" is the nervous system of the economy, constantly sensing and responding.

The system also provides the gift of transformation, or liquidity. Imagine if your house was your only savings. To buy groceries, you'd have to sell a window or a few bricks—an impossible situation. The financial system allows you to hold your wealth in forms, like stocks or bonds, that can be converted back into cash almost instantly. It's a kind of financial alchemy that turns solid, long-term investments into spendable cash when you need it. This freedom gives us the confidence to invest for the future, knowing the present is still within reach.

Furthermore, it's our civilization's master weaver of safety nets. Life is a tightrope walk over a canyon of uncertainty. The financial system allows us to weave a net below. Insurance is the most obvious thread, protecting us from the sudden storms of accident or illness. But there are more complex tools, like derivatives, that let a farmer lock in a price for their crop before it's even harvested, ensuring a hailstorm doesn't wipe out their year's income. By sharing and managing risk, the system helps us all walk the tightrope with a little more courage.

And finally, it is the invisible, tireless courier. Every tap of your card, every bill you pay online, every paycheck that appears in your account—these are small miracles of trust and technology. The financial system is the silent, behind-the-scenes infrastructure that processes trillions of these transactions a day, ensuring that the simple act of exchange happens flawlessly. It's the humble, foundational work that allows the entire grand ballet of the economy to proceed.

2. A Tour of the Financial Kingdom: Assets and Their Arenas

To truly understand the world of finance, think of it as a vast and ancient kingdom. This kingdom is filled with treasures of all kinds (assets) and sprawling marketplaces where they are traded (markets).

The kingdom's treasures can be divided into two fundamental types.

First, there are the Real Assets. These are the tangible, physical treasures of the kingdom. They are the castles and land (real estate), the iron forges and looms (machinery), the gold in the royal vault and the wheat in the fields (commodities). You can touch them, see them, and use them. Their value comes from their physical substance and what they can do. They are the bedrock of the kingdom's wealth.

Then, there are the Financial Assets. These are the kingdom's magic scrolls and royal decrees. They have no physical form, but they hold immense power. A financial asset is a promise, a claim on a future treasure. A stock certificate is like a deed granting you a share of a merchant ship's future profits. A bond is a solemn IOU from the King, promising to repay a loan with interest. These enchanted scrolls are what allow the kingdom's wealth to flow and grow in complex ways.

Now, let's visit the kingdom's marketplaces, or Markets.

We can map them by the treasures sold there. The Stock Market is the Grand Bazaar, a chaotic and vibrant square where deeds to the kingdom's greatest ventures (companies) are shouted, bartered, and traded. The Bond Market is the quiet, stately Royal Treasury, where the IOUs of the King and his noble houses are traded with sober gravity. The Foreign Exchange Market is the bustling port city, where the currencies of all the world's kingdoms are exchanged to fuel international trade. And the Commodities Market is like the vast guildhalls of the farmers and miners, where the future value of wheat, oil, and gold is debated and decided.

We can also classify markets by the length of their promises. The Money Market is the fast-paced, short-term lending square. It's where merchants and nobles get quick loans to cover expenses for a week or a month, using highly trusted, easily exchanged notes. Think of it as the kingdom's payday lender. The Capital Market is where the grand, long-term visions are funded. This is where you finance a cathedral that will take decades to build or fund an expedition to a new continent. It deals in stocks and long-term bonds—the financial tools for building legacies.

Finally, every market has two distinct areas. The Primary Market is the Royal Mint or the Scribe's Guild—it's where new treasures are forged. When a company first offers its stock to the public (an IPO), it's like a new ship being christened and its ownership deeds sold for the first time. The money goes directly to fund the voyage. The Secondary Market, where most of the action happens, is the vast network of streets and exchanges where those deeds are then traded between citizens. The original voyager doesn't get any more money; instead, ownership simply passes from one hand to another, giving everyone the confidence to invest in the first place, knowing they can always find a buyer later.

3. The Royal Armory: A Guide to Financial Instruments

Step into the financial kingdom's armory and treasury. Here you will find the powerful tools, enchanted items, and core elements that shape fortunes and build empires.

Securities: The Scrolls of Ownership & Debt

These are formal contracts representing a claim to value.

Equity Securities (Stocks): Think of these as a deed to a small plot of a company's kingdom. You are now a part-owner, entitled to a share of the profits (dividends) and a voice in its governance.

Common Stock: The standard deed. It gives you voting rights—a say in how the kingdom is run—and a claim to whatever is left if the company is ever sold off. Its value can soar to the heavens or fall to dust.

Preferred Stock: A deed with a royal seal. You usually give up your right to vote, but in exchange, you receive a fixed, regular payment, and you get paid before the common folk if the company falters. It's a hybrid of safety and potential.

Debt Securities (Bonds): This is a solemn IOU, a formal promise of debt. You lend money to a government or a company, and they promise to pay you back in full on a specific date (maturity), making regular interest payments (coupons) along the way as a thank you.

Government Bonds: An IOU from the King himself (e.g., U.S. Treasury bonds). Considered the safest promise in the land.

Corporate Bonds: An IOU from a great merchant house or guild. The riskier the company, the more interest they must promise to make the loan worthwhile.

Currencies: The Blood of Commerce

These are the accepted mediums of exchange, the very coins of the realm.

Fiat Currencies: Think of the U.S. Dollar (USD) or the Euro (EUR). Their value isn't based on the gold they're made of, but on the strength and stability of the kingdom that issues them. They work because we all believe they do.

Cryptocurrencies: A new, rebellious form of currency, like Bitcoin (BTC). It's a "ghost coin," not issued by any king, but mined from pure mathematics and secured by a decentralized network of scribes. Its value is volatile, a frontier of finance.

Contracts: The Binding Spells of Finance

These are agreements that derive their power from other assets.

Derivatives: These are financial shadow puppets. Their value isn't their own; it's derived from the shape of an underlying asset, like a stock, a commodity, or an interest rate. They are used to hedge against risk or to make speculative bets.

Futures & Forwards: A binding handshake to buy or sell something at a set price on a future date. It's like a farmer agreeing in the spring to sell his wheat for a fixed price at harvest, no matter what the market price is then.

Options: A more flexible spell. It gives you the right, but not the obligation, to buy or sell an asset at a set price. It's like buying a ticket that gives you the option to see the show, but you don't have to go if you decide against it.

Commodities: The Earth's Bounty

These are the raw, untamed materials of the world, traded in bulk.

Energy: The fire and fuel of the modern world—crude oil, natural gas.

Metals: The dragon's hoard of precious metals like gold and silver (a safe harbor in uncertain times) and the foundational industrial metals like copper and aluminum (the building blocks of progress).

Agricultural: The bounty of the harvest—wheat, corn, coffee, and sugar. Their prices are at the mercy of weather, pests, and human taste.

Real Assets: The Tangible Kingdom

These are the physical treasures you can stand on, live in, and touch.

Real Estate: Your personal castle keep, your plot of land. It can provide shelter, income through rent, and a lasting store of value.

Infrastructure: The great public works of the kingdom—its roads, bridges, and aqueducts. These are long-term investments that serve everyone and provide steady, reliable returns.

Collectibles: Unique treasures whose value is driven by scarcity and passion—a master's painting, a vintage car, a rare stamp. They are investments of the heart as much as the mind.

4. The Cast of Characters: The Movers and Shakers of Finance

The financial system isn't just an abstract network; it's powered by a diverse cast of characters and guilds, known as financial intermediaries. They are the essential matchmakers, guides, and guardians who stand between savers and borrowers, making the whole system work for the rest of us.

The Depository Guild: The Keepers of Coin

These are the most familiar faces in the financial kingdom. They take your money for safekeeping (deposits) and lend it out to others.

Commercial Banks: The ubiquitous town banker. They are the jacks-of-all-trades, offering a safe place for your gold (checking/savings accounts), providing loans for everything from a new horse to a new business, and handling the daily flow of commerce.

Credit Unions: The friendly neighborhood cooperative. Owned by their members, they offer the same services as a bank but often with a more personal touch, better rates, and a mission to serve a specific community rather than to maximize profit.

The Contractual Guild: The Planners and Protectors

These characters operate on long-term promises, collecting regular fees in exchange for future security.

Insurance Companies: The Guild of Shield-Bearers. You pay them a small, regular fee (a premium), and in return, they promise to stand with you and absorb the financial blow of a catastrophe—a fire, a shipwreck, an illness. They pool the kingdom's risk, making life's uncertainties more bearable for everyone.

Pension Funds: The Wardens of Tomorrow. They are the loyal guardians of your retirement savings. They collect and invest contributions throughout your working life, managing them over decades to ensure you have a steady stream of income in your golden years.

The Investment Guild: The Architects and Adventurers

This guild is focused on building wealth, funding grand projects, and navigating the high-stakes world of investment.

Investment Banks: The master architects of the financial world. They don't serve everyday folk, but kings and giant merchant guilds. They design and build the financial bridges for massive projects, like helping a company sell ownership deeds for the first time (an IPO) or advising one king on how to merge his realm with another (M&A).

Mutual Funds: The savvy caravan masters. For a small fee, they allow you to place your goods (money) into their large, well-defended convoy. The caravan master (a professional manager) invests the pooled money in a wide variety of ventures, giving you the benefit of diversification and expertise you couldn't achieve alone.

Hedge Funds: The secretive leagues of elite mercenaries. They serve only the wealthiest patrons and use complex, high-risk strategies (the financial world's equivalent of espionage and flanking maneuvers) in an attempt to achieve spectacular returns, unbound by the rules that govern ordinary caravans.

Venture Capital Firms: The bold explorers. They are the patrons who fund the risky expeditions to the edge of the map. They provide gold and guidance to young, unproven inventors and startups, betting that one of them will discover a new continent of immense value. They are the funders of the future.

1. The Investor's Compass: Choosing Your Market Direction

Think of investing not just as buying something, but as making a prediction about the future. It's like being a weather forecaster for money. The "position" you take is your forecast—are you predicting sunshine or a storm for a particular stock, bond, or commodity? This forecast determines how you'll navigate the market and is the key to both your potential success and the storms you might have to weather.

The most intuitive forecast is betting on a sunny day. This is a long position. You buy an asset because you believe in it. You've done your homework, you like its story, and you expect its value to rise, basking in the warmth of a growing market. It's the classic tale of "buy low, sell high." You own it, you hold it, and you hope its price climbs toward the sun. If you buy 100 shares of a company at $50 each, and it later blossoms to $60, you've earned a nice $1,000 for your optimism. This is the bedrock of most investing—a fundamental belief that good things will grow over time. The risk? An unexpected cold front; if the price drops, your investment shivers.

But what if you see dark clouds gathering? What if you believe an asset is overvalued and destined for a downpour? You can take a short position. This is a more complex maneuver, like opening an umbrella before it starts to rain. You're betting on a price drop. Here's the magic trick: you borrow the asset from someone (like your broker), sell it immediately at its current high price, and wait. If you're right and the price tumbles, you buy it back at the new, lower price and return it to the lender. The difference is your profit. Imagine shorting 100 shares at $100 each. The price plummets to $80. You swoop in, buy them back for $8,000, and return them, pocketing a cool $2,000. The danger here is immense: what if you forecast rain, but a heatwave hits instead? The price could skyrocket indefinitely, and your potential loss is, theoretically, limitless. It's a high-stakes game of meteorological finance.

Then there's the world of derivatives, which are like advanced weather-predicting instruments. Buying a call option is like buying a ticket for an outdoor concert with a rain date. You get the right, but not the obligation, to buy an asset at a set price. If the sun shines (price goes up), you use your ticket and enjoy the show. If it rains (price goes down), you can just let the ticket expire, losing only the small amount you paid for it. Conversely, a put option is like buying insurance on that concert ticket. It gives you the right to sell at a set price, protecting you from a washout (a price drop).

Finally, you have futures contracts, which are less like a forecast and more like a binding promise. Taking a long futures position means you agree, right now, to buy an asset on a specific day in the future at a price you set today. A short futures position means you agree to sell. It's like pre-ordering next year's harvest at today's prices. Whether a drought or a bumper crop comes, you're locked in.

Ultimately, your choice of position is your personal market story. Are you an optimist planting seeds for the long term, a skeptic preparing for a storm, or a strategist using advanced tools to play the changing weather?

2. The Art of the Margin: A Financial Power-Up

Imagine you're in a race, and you have the option to hit a turbo-boost button. That's essentially what margin trading is: using borrowed funds from your broker to amplify your investment power. But like any good power-up, it magnifies everything—the speed, the thrill, and the crash. Understanding the numbers behind it is your dashboard for keeping this powerful engine under control.

First up is the Leverage Ratio. Think of this as your "magnification dial." It tells you how much bigger your financial footprint is compared to the money you actually put down. The formula is simple:

Leverage Ratio=Your Own Equity Total Value of Asset

So, if you want to buy $10,000 worth of stock but only use $5,000 of your own cash (borrowing the other $5,000), your dial is set to 2.0x ($10,000 / 5,000). You're controlling twice the amount of capital you personally committed. A higher number means a more aggressive boost, making the scenery—and the risks—fly by that much faster.

Next, let's look at the Rate of Return. This is the scoreboard that tells you how well your turbo-boost paid off. It's not just about how much the stock went up; it's about how much your personal stake grew, after paying for the borrowed fuel. The calculation looks like this:

Rate of Return=Your Initial Equity (Profit from Sale−Interest Paid−Commissions)

Let's bring back our $10,000 position. Say it zooms to $12,000, giving you a $2,000 profit. You paid $100 in interest and fees. Your net profit is $1,900. Your return isn't on the full $10,000, but on the $5,000 you actually invested. That's a whopping 38% return ($1,900 / 5,000). Without the margin boost, your $5,000 would have only made $1,000 (a 20% return). See the amplification? But remember, this magnifying glass works both ways; a drop in price would have created a much steeper percentage loss on your personal cash.

Finally, the most critical number: the Margin Call Price. This is the "danger zone" alarm. Your broker, who lent you the money, needs to know their loan is safe. If the value of your investment drops too low, they'll "call" you, demanding you either add more of your own cash or sell assets to cover the risk. This is the price point where the warning lights flash. Here's the formula that sets off the alarm:

Margin Call Price=1−Maintenance Margin Requirement Amount Borrowed per Share

Let's say you borrowed $5,000 to buy 100 shares at $100 each (so you borrowed $50 per share), and your broker's maintenance margin is 30% (or 0.30). The price that triggers a call is:

1−0.30$50=0.70$50≈$71.43 per share

If your stock's price falls to $71.43, your phone will ring. Your broker isn't being mean; they're protecting themselves from your turbo-boosted crash. Understanding this number isn't just math—it's your survival guide to using financial leverage without getting burned.

3. The Anatomy of a Trade: Giving Your Broker a Game Plan

Placing a trade is like sending a secret agent on a mission. You don't just tell them what to get; you give them a detailed briefing on how, when, and what to do with it afterwards. These instructions are your game plan, and they fall into three categories: execution, validity, and clearing.

Execution instructions are the "Rules of Engagement." This is how you want your agent to carry out the mission. Do they go in loud or quiet?

An "All-or-None" (AON) order is like telling your agent, "Secure all ten briefcases, or abort the mission." It prevents you from ending up with just a few, which might not be what you wanted.

A "Fill-or-Kill" (FOK) order is even more demanding: "Get all ten briefcases right now, in one go, or the deal is off." It's for when timing is absolutely critical.

An "Immediate-or-Cancel" (IOC) order is a bit more flexible: "Grab as many briefcases as you can in this instant. Abort the mission for any you can't get immediately." You'll take what you can get, right now. These instructions are about controlling the process of the trade, ensuring it happens on your terms.

Validity instructions are the "Mission Timeline." This is when your order is live and active. Is the mission for today only, or is it a long-term surveillance operation?

A "Day Order" is the default: "This mission is valid until the market closes today. If you haven't completed it by then, come home."

A "Good-till-Canceled" (GTC) order is for the patient player: "Your mission stands until I call you off or you succeed." You might set a price target and be willing to wait for weeks, letting your agent lie in wait for the perfect moment to strike. (Brokers usually put a 60- or 90-day limit on this so your agent doesn't stay in the field forever).

"At-the-Open" or "At-the-Close" orders are precise: "Execute this mission precisely at the opening bell" or "...at the closing bell." You're targeting a specific moment of the day, for strategic reasons.

This is about controlling the lifespan of your order, so it doesn't expire before its time or linger when it's no longer relevant.

Finally, clearing instructions are the "Extraction Plan." This is the administrative backend—what happens after the mission is a success. It's about getting the asset (the security) and the payment (the money) to the right places. For most individual investors, this is handled automatically by the broker. But for big institutions, it's like specifying which secret bank account the funds should be wired to and which secure warehouse the asset should be delivered to. It's the behind-the-scenes logistics that ensure that after all the action, the goods are safely transferred and the books are balanced.

In short: Execution is the how. Validity is the when. Clearing is the where to next. Mastering them turns a simple "buy" or "sell" command into a finely tuned strategic operation.

4. The Trader's Dilemma: Speed vs. Price

When you step up to the plate to make a trade, you face a fundamental choice that defines your entire strategy: Do you want it done now, or do you want it done at your price? This is the core difference between a market order and a limit order. It's a classic battle of speed versus control.

A market order is the "Get it done NOW" button. You're telling the market, "I want to buy (or sell) this security immediately, and I'll take whatever the best price is at this very second." Its superpower is speed and certainty of execution. If a stock is in freefall and you want out, a market order is your parachute—it will get you out of the plane instantly. The trade-off? You give up all control over the price. The price you saw a second ago might not be the price you get. In a chaotic, fast-moving market, this gap, known as "slippage," can feel like jumping from a plane and landing a few blocks away from your target. You're guaranteed an exit, but the landing spot is a bit of a surprise.

A limit order, on the other hand, is the tool of the patient strategist. You're telling the market, "I have my terms." For a buyer, it's: "I'm willing to buy this stock, but only if the price drops to $50 or less." For a seller, it's: "I'm happy to sell, but not for a penny less than $55." Its superpower is absolute price control. You will never pay more or receive less than you specified. This protects you from slippage and lets you execute your strategy with precision, waiting for the market to come to you. The trade-off? Execution is not guaranteed. Your order might sit there, unfulfilled, as the stock price merrily dances just out of your reach. You wanted to buy at $50, but it never dipped below $51 before soaring to the moon. You protected your price, but you missed the rocket ship entirely.

So, what's the choice?

Go with a Market Order when your priority is immediate action. You need in or out, and a few cents difference in price is less important than the certainty of the trade itself. Think of it as hailing a cab in the rain—you'll take the first one that stops, regardless of the fare.

Go with a Limit Order when your priority is price. You have a specific value in mind, and you're willing to risk missing the trade to avoid paying too much or selling for too little. It's like setting a silent auction bid—you name your price and wait to see if you win.

The choice isn't just technical; it's philosophical. Are you a sprinter who values speed, or a sniper who values precision? Your answer will tell you which order is right for you.

From Blueprint to Bustling Metropolis: A Tale of Two Markets

Every great company, every big idea, needs fuel. That fuel is capital. But where does it come from? It all starts in the world of financial markets, which isn't one monolithic thing but a dynamic ecosystem with two distinct, yet deeply connected, realms: the primary market and the secondary market.

The Primary Market: The Delivery Room 👶

Imagine a brilliant startup, "Innovate Inc.," has a game-changing idea but empty pockets. They need to raise cash to build their dream. So, they step into the primary market. This is the birthplace of new securities. It's where companies, for the very first time, offer brand-new stocks or bonds to the public.

An Initial Public Offering (IPO) is the celebrity version of this. Innovate Inc. "goes public," selling its first-ever shares to investors. It's like the grand opening of a new business, with a massive influx of cash to get things rolling.

Think of the primary market as the architect's blueprint and construction phase. It's where the initial funds are raised, the foundation is laid, and the company gets the resources it needs to grow. The money goes directly from the investor's wallet to the company's bank account.

The Secondary Market: The City That Never Sleeps 🏙️

Once Innovate Inc.'s shares are born in the primary market, they don't just sit there. They move out into the secondary market—think the New York Stock Exchange (NYSE) or NASDAQ. This is the sprawling, bustling city where those shares now live. It's a vibrant marketplace where investors trade existing securities among themselves.

When you buy a share of Apple on your phone, you're not giving money to Apple; you're buying it from another investor who decided to sell. The company isn't directly involved in the transaction at all.

So, if the company doesn't get the money, why is the secondary market so important? Because it's the entire reason the primary market can exist.

Imagine buying a brand-new car (a primary market transaction) but being told you could never, ever sell it. You'd probably hesitate, right? The secondary market is the ultimate used-car lot, the global StubHub, the escape hatch. It provides:

Liquidity: The confidence that you can sell your investment whenever you want. This makes people far more willing to take a chance on a new company in the primary market.

Price Discovery: The constant buying and selling in the secondary market sets a real-time price tag on a company's stock. It's the wisdom of the crowd, telling Innovate Inc. (and the world) what its shares are worth at any given moment.

Without the promise of a lively, liquid secondary market, the primary market would be a ghost town. No one would show up for the grand opening if they knew the doors would lock behind them forever.

The Three Flavors of Trading: How Deals Get Done

So how does all this buying and selling actually happen? It's not always a chaotic free-for-all. Trading unfolds in different arenas, each with its own vibe.

1. The Quote-Driven Market: The Art Gallery Deal

Think of this as a high-end art gallery or a vintage car dealership. A dealer (often a big bank) owns the inventory (stocks, bonds, currencies). They post two prices: a bid price (what they'll pay you for your asset) and an ask price (what you'll have to pay them). The difference, the bid-ask spread, is their profit.

You walk in, you talk to the dealer, and you make a deal. It's common in the foreign exchange (FX) and bond markets. It's perfect for unique or less-common items because the dealer provides the liquidity, always ready to make a market. The downside? It's not always transparent; you only see that one dealer's prices.

2. The Order-Driven Market: The Grand Central Auction 🏛

This is the market you see in the movies—a giant, electronic auction house like the NYSE or NASDAQ. Everyone's buy and sell orders are thrown into one central, transparent system.

An algorithm then plays matchmaker, connecting the highest buy order with the lowest sell order. It's all based on price and time priority: the best price gets matched first. It's fast, efficient, and incredibly transparent, which is why it works so well for popular, high-volume stocks like those of tech giants and blue-chip companies.

3. The Brokered Market: The Super-Connector 🤝

What if you're trying to sell something massive and unique, like an entire city block or a one-of-a-kind, complex derivative? You don't go to an auction; you call a broker.

In a brokered market, the broker is a master networker. They don't buy or sell anything themselves. Their job is to find the perfect counterparty for a difficult trade, connecting a specific buyer with a specific seller. They are the ultimate matchmakers for the big, bespoke, and illiquid deals that happen behind the scenes, earning a commission for their expert service.

The Anatomy of a Healthy Financial System 💪

A truly well-functioning financial system is like a healthy human body. It's a marvel of efficiency, resilience, and interconnected parts working in harmony to fuel the economy. Here's what it looks like:

An Efficient Heart (Capital Allocation): It pumps money (capital) from savers to the businesses and innovators who can use it most productively, just as a heart pumps oxygen-rich blood where it's needed most.

Clear Vision (Transparency): Everyone has access to timely, accurate information. Think of it as perfect 20/20 vision, where investors can clearly see the risks and opportunities, preventing them from stumbling in the dark.

A Fast Metabolism (Liquidity & Price Discovery): Assets can be converted to cash quickly without losing value, and prices react instantly to new information. The system processes news and transactions with lightning speed.

A Strong Skeleton (Regulation & Legal System): Robust rules and enforceable contracts provide the structure and support. They protect investors from fraud, ensure promises are kept, and prevent the whole system from collapsing under stress.

An Adaptive Immune System (Risk Management): It has sophisticated tools (like derivatives and insurance) to manage, hedge, and transfer risk. It can fight off infections (market shocks) and has contingency plans (crisis management) to prevent a small problem from becoming a pandemic.

When all these systems are humming, they create a climate of trust and confidence that encourages investment, powers innovation, and drives prosperity for everyone.

The Rulebook: Why We Need Referees in the Market

Without rules, any game descends into chaos. Market regulation isn't about stifling growth; it's about making sure the game is fair, safe, and sustainable for everyone. The referees of the financial world (like the SEC in the U.S.) have a few key goals:

Protect the Players (Investor Protection): This is Rule #1. Regulations are there to shield investors from cheats, liars, and manipulators. They fight against things like insider trading (playing with a stacked deck) and outright fraud to ensure a level playing field.

Keep the Game Running Smoothly (Market Integrity): The goal is to ensure the market is orderly and prices are fair. This includes things like "circuit breakers" that pause trading during a panic, preventing a stampede from turning into a total collapse.

Prevent a League-Wide Collapse (Mitigating Systemic Risk): This is the big one. Regulators work to prevent the failure of one massive institution from creating a domino effect that takes down the entire financial system (think the 2008 crisis). They do this by requiring banks to have thick safety cushions (capital requirements) and keeping a close eye on how interconnected everyone is.

Fight Crime (Anti-Money Laundering): The financial system can't be a playground for criminals. Strict rules are in place to prevent money laundering and the financing of illegal activities, protecting the integrity of the market from those who want to abuse it.

Security Market Indexes

The Market's Heartbeat: Listening to the Story of Indices

The financial world is a cacophony. Thousands of companies, millions of trades, a constant barrage of news—it's a chaotic symphony of human ambition and fear. Trying to make sense of it all by watching every single stock would be like trying to understand a city's mood by listening to every single conversation at once. It's impossible. So how do we find the melody in the noise? We listen to the market's heartbeat. We look to security market indices.

These indices are the EKG of the economy, distilling the frantic, complex rhythm of the entire market into a single, vital pulse. They are our guides, our storytellers. An index is a curated collection, a fantasy portfolio of securities chosen to represent a specific slice of the world—the all-stars of a country's economy, the rising talent in the tech sector, or the steady veterans of industry. Think of the S&P 500. It's not just a list of 500 companies; it's the varsity team for American business. When its value climbs, it tells a story of confidence and growth. When it falls, it whispers of caution and retreat.

For investors, these indices are the North Star. They're the benchmark against which we measure our own journeys. Is your portfolio keeping pace with the market's stars, or is it time to rethink the game plan? For the architects of our economy—the central banks and governments—indices are the weather report, helping them see if a storm is brewing or if clear skies are ahead, guiding policies that affect us all. They are the silent conductors of the financial orchestra, turning chaos into a story we can understand, a pulse we can follow.

The Story Behind the Numbers: Price vs. Total Return

To truly understand the story an index is telling, we need to learn its language. This means looking beyond a simple "up" or "down" and understanding how its value and returns are born.

The Index Value: A Fair Game

Imagine you're managing a fantasy sports team. The team's "value" is simply the combined score of all your players. This is the essence of a price-weighted index. You add up the stock prices of all the companies in the index and divide by a special number called a divisor.
Let's say your team has three players with scores:

Player A: 50 points

Player B: 100 points

Player C: 150 points

Your team's value is \$50 + \$100 + 150=300.

But what happens if Player A has a 2-for-1 stock split? Their price tag drops to \$25, but their underlying value hasn't changed. To keep the game fair and prevent your team's value from artificially crashing, the referee (the index manager) adjusts the divisor. The new sum is \$25 + \$100 + 150=275. To keep the value at 300, the divisor is changed from 1.0 to 0.9167. This adjustment is the secret sauce that lets us compare the index's performance fairly over decades, through splits, mergers, and player trades.

Most modern indices, like the S&P 500, use a market-capitalization weighting, which is more like a team where the MVP's points count for more. A company's influence is based on its total market value (price multiplied by number of shares), giving a truer picture of its economic muscle.

Price Return: The Headline Story

Price Return is the number you see in the headlines. It's the raw, unadorned change in the index's value based purely on price movements. It's the capital gain, the simple story of how much the sticker price of your investment went up or down.

The formula is straightforward:
Price Return=Beginning Index Value(Ending Index Value−Beginning Index Value)

If an index starts at 1,000 points and ends at 1,010, the price return is a clean 1%.
1000(1010−1000)=0.01 or 1%

It's a useful snapshot, but it's not the whole story.

Total Return: The Real Story

Total Return is the director's cut. It's the full, rich narrative of an investment's performance because it includes the secret ingredient to long-term wealth: dividends. Dividends are like small, periodic cash bonuses that companies pay out to their shareholders. Total return assumes you take those bonuses and immediately reinvest them, buying more shares and allowing your wealth to compound.

The formula adds this crucial piece:
Total Return=Beginning Index Value(Ending Index Value−Beginning Index Value+Income from Securities)

Let's go back to our index. It went from 1,000 to 1,010. But let's say the companies within it paid out dividends that, if reinvested, would be worth 5 index points.
1000(1010−1000+5)=0.015 or 1.5%

That extra 0.5% might seem small, but over years and decades, the magic of compounding dividends can be the difference between a good investment and a life-changing one. While the price return tells you what the market did, the total return tells you what you earned.

The Curator's Craft: Building and Maintaining an Index

Creating an index isn't just math; it's an art. It's the work of a skilled curator, carefully selecting and maintaining a collection that tells a true and compelling story about the market.

The Blueprint: Defining the Exhibit

The first step is deciding what story to tell. Is this an exhibit on "The Titans of American Industry" (a large-cap index)? Or a showcase of "The Innovators of Tomorrow" (a tech sector index)? Or a grand, sweeping collection of "Global Commerce"? This decision defines the universe of potential candidates and sets the theme for the entire collection.

The Audition: Selecting the Stars

Once the theme is set, the casting call begins. Not every company gets a spot in the exhibit. They must audition, meeting strict criteria:

Stature (Market Capitalization): The company has to be big enough to matter.

Star Power (Liquidity): Its shares must be traded frequently, ensuring its price is a true reflection of public sentiment, not a fluke.

Public Access (Public Float): A significant portion of its shares must be available to the public, not locked away by insiders. This ensures the company's performance reflects the experience of everyday investors.

Genre (Sector): The company must fit the theme of the exhibit. A bank wouldn't be cast in a healthcare-focused index.

The number of stars is also key. Too few, and the story is incomplete. Too many, and the exhibit becomes a cluttered mess. The S&P 500's curators chose 500 to strike a powerful balance, capturing over 80% of the U.S. market's value in a manageable cast.

Keeping the Story Fresh: Rebalancing and Reconstitution

An index is a living museum, not a dusty attic. As the market story evolves, the exhibit must change with it. This happens in two ways:

Rebalancing: This is like adjusting the lighting on the artworks. Over time, as some companies grow faster than others, their weights in the index can get out of sync. Rebalancing gently nudges those weights back to the curator's original blueprint.

Reconstitution: This is the big one—changing the art on the walls. Fading stars are removed, and new, rising stars that meet the audition criteria are brought in. This ensures the index remains a relevant, up-to-date reflection of the market, not a tribute to yesterday's heroes.

This curatorial process is fraught with challenges. The curator must avoid survivorship bias—the trap of telling history by only looking at the winners, ignoring the companies that failed and vanished. This would paint an overly rosy picture of the past. They must rely on transparent, published rules so that everyone, from a fund manager to a curious student, can understand how the story is being told. It's this blend of scientific rigor and artistic curation that makes an index a trusted narrator of the financial world.

The Weight of a Vote: How Influence is Measured in the Market

Imagine the market is a grand democracy. How do we decide whose voice matters most? The "weighting method" of an index is its system of governance—it determines which companies get the most say in shaping the index's story.

1. Price-Weighted: The Loudest Voice Wins

This is the oldest system, a bit like an old town hall where the person who shouts the loudest gets the most attention. A stock's influence is based purely on its share price. A $200 stock has twice the pull of a $100 stock, even if the company behind the $100 stock is ten times larger and more important to the economy.

Famous Examples: The Dow Jones Industrial Average (DJIA), the elder statesman of indices, still uses this method.

The Upside: It's wonderfully simple.

The Downside: It's arbitrary. A company's stock price is a function of its history, including stock splits. A great company that splits its stock to make it more affordable for small investors would see its voice in the index immediately diminished. It's a system that values a high price tag over true economic substance.

2. Market-Cap-Weighted: One Dollar, One Vote

This is the dominant system of governance in the modern financial world. A company's influence is proportional to its total market value (its "market capitalization"). It's a system of economic democracy: the bigger and more valuable you are, the more votes you get.

Famous Examples: The S&P 500, the MSCI World, and nearly every major global benchmark.

The Upside: It's a mirror. It reflects the reality of the market, where massive companies like Apple or Amazon have a much larger impact than smaller firms. It captures the world as it is.

The Downside: It can lead to an oligarchy. The index can become top-heavy, dominated by a handful of mega-companies. If a few tech giants have a bad day, they can drag the entire market story down with them, even if hundreds of smaller companies are thriving. It also has a tendency to "buy high," giving more weight to stocks after they've already had a huge run-up in price.

3. Equal-Weighted: One Company, One Vote

This is the purest form of democracy. Every company in the index, from the global behemoth to the promising upstart, gets exactly one vote. Their influence is identical.

Famous Example: The S&P 500 Equal Weight Index.

The Upside: It's the ultimate diversification. It reduces the risk of being dominated by a few giants and gives a bigger voice to smaller and mid-sized companies, which often have more room to grow. It's a bet on the underdog.

The Downside: It's high-maintenance. To keep every voice equal, the index must be constantly rebalanced—selling some of the winners who have grown too loud and buying more of the underperformers to amplify their voices. This can lead to higher trading costs. It's also an idealized view; in the real world, a corner store doesn't have the same economic impact as Walmart.

There is no single "right" way to count the votes. Each method tells a different story, offering a unique perspective on the market's character. Understanding which system of governance an index uses is the final key to deciphering its message and choosing the narrator that best aligns with your own investment philosophy.

How a Stock Market Index is Like a Playlist 🎵

Ever wonder what a stock market index like the S&P 500 actually is? Forget the dry-as-dust definitions. Think of an index as a playlist for the economy. Its job is to capture the vibe of a specific corner of the market. But how you build that playlist—which songs you choose and how loud you play them—changes everything. This is called the "weighting method."

Price-Weighted: The Loudest Song Wins

Imagine a playlist where the song with the highest track number (e.g., Track #99) gets the most attention, regardless of whether it's a hit song or an obscure B-side. That's a price-weighted index. The stock with the highest price-per-share has the most pull.

The Dow Jones Industrial Average (DJIA) is the classic example. It's like a jukebox that's influenced more by a $300 stock from a medium-sized company than a $50 stock from a global giant. It's simple, but it can feel a bit random, like letting the loudest person in the room dictate the conversation.

Market Cap-Weighted: The Superstar Effect

This is the most popular way to build an index, and it's like a Spotify Top Hits playlist. The biggest, most popular artists (companies with the highest market capitalization—their total value) get the most airtime.

The S&P 500 works this way. Mega-companies like Apple and Microsoft are the Taylor Swifts and Drakes of the index; their performance defines the playlist's overall feel. If they have a great day, the whole index bops along. This makes sense because it reflects where most of the money in the market actually is. The downside? If a few superstars are having a bad day, they can drown out a chorus of smaller, thriving companies.

Equal-Weighted: The Perfect Mixtape

Remember making a mixtape for a friend, carefully giving every artist one song to shine? That's an equal-weighted index. Every single company in the index, whether it's a garage band or a stadium-filler, gets the exact same slice of the pie.

This method gives smaller companies a real voice and avoids having the whole index swayed by a few giants. It's like giving everyone at a party the same amount of time on the karaoke machine. The catch is that it requires constant tweaking (or "rebalancing") to make sure everyone's share stays equal as their fortunes rise and fall.

Fundamental-Weighted: The Critic's Choice

This is the thinking person's playlist. Instead of price or popularity, stocks are weighted by their fundamentals—their financial health. Think strong sales, solid profits, or juicy dividends.

It's like a music critic creating a "Best Of" list based on lyrical genius and musical composition, not just radio plays. The idea is to find true, intrinsic value, not just what's currently hyped. It's a fantastic concept for investors who believe that, in the long run, quality wins out over popularity.

The Index's Gardeners: Rebalancing and Reconstitution 🌿

An index isn't a "set it and forget it" affair. To stay relevant, it needs regular maintenance, kind of like a garden. This upkeep comes in two forms: rebalancing and reconstitution.

Rebalancing: Pruning the Hedges

Rebalancing is the act of trimming and tending to the plants already in your garden to maintain its intended design.

Imagine you designed your garden to have an equal mix of roses, tulips, and daisies (like an equal-weighted index). Over time, the roses might grow like crazy, overshadowing everything else. Rebalancing is the process of pruning those overgrown roses and using the clippings to nurture the smaller daisies and tulips, bringing the garden back to its original, balanced look.

For a cap-weighted index, this is less about pruning and more about just letting the big trees get bigger. But for equal-weighted and fundamental-weighted indexes, this regular tidying is crucial to keeping the index true to its philosophy. It creates a built-in "sell high, buy low" discipline.

Reconstitution: Weeding and Planting Anew

Reconstitution is more dramatic. It's about changing the very plants in the garden. It's the process of yanking out the weeds and planting new, promising seedlings.

Markets change. Companies get acquired, go bankrupt, or just don't fit the index's theme anymore. Meanwhile, new and exciting companies pop up. The committee that manages an index will periodically review its members and kick some out while inviting others in.

When a company gets added to a major index like the S&P 500, it's like a small-town band getting a headlining slot at Coachella. Suddenly, every index fund has to buy its stock, causing a rush of demand. This is the "index effect," and it shows just how much influence these behind-the-scenes gardening decisions can have.

Why We Can't Live Without Indexes: The Swiss Army Knife of Finance 🛠️

Indexes are far more than just a scorekeeper for the market. They are one of the most versatile tools in the financial world, serving a bunch of essential jobs.

The Scorecard (Benchmarking): This is their most famous job. An index is the ultimate yardstick. Are you, an investor, beating the market? You can only know by comparing your portfolio's return to a relevant benchmark, like the S&P 500. It keeps everyone—from amateur investors to highly-paid fund managers—honest.

The Weather Report (Market Proxy): Want a quick read on the economy's mood? Look at a broad market index. A rising index is like a sunny forecast, signaling optimism and confidence. A falling index suggests stormy weather ahead. It gives you the big picture without you having to check on thousands of individual companies.

The Blueprint (Basis for Investments): The entire passive investing revolution is built on indexes. Index funds and ETFs are like master chefs who take the index's recipe and replicate it perfectly. By buying one share of an S&P 500 ETF, you get a tiny slice of 500 of America's biggest companies. It's diversification made easy.

The Crystal Ball (Gauging Sentiment): Indexes are a powerful gauge of human emotion—specifically, the twin drivers of markets: greed and fear. A soaring index reflects widespread optimism (a "bull market"), while a plunging one signals panic (a "bear market").

Exploring the Neighborhoods of the Stock Market

Not all indexes are the same. They're like guidebooks to different neighborhoods in the vast, sprawling city of the stock market. Knowing which neighborhood you want to visit is key to any investment strategy.

Broad Market Indexes (The City Skyline): These give you the panoramic, postcard view of an entire country's market. Think of the Wilshire 5000 in the U.S. or the FTSE All-Share in the U.K. They try to capture everything.

Style Indexes (Growth vs. Value): Are you headed to the flashy, futuristic tech district, full of sleek skyscrapers and a "grow-at-all-costs" vibe? That's a Growth Index. Or do you prefer the historic old town, with its sturdy, reliable buildings that have stood for ages and pay regular rent (dividends)? That's a Value Index.

Size Indexes (The Districts): You can also tour the city based on the size of its buildings.

Large-Cap: The skyscraper district, home to the biggest, most famous corporate titans (S&P 100).

Mid-Cap: The bustling midtown, full of dynamic companies that are big but still have room to grow (S&P MidCap 400).

Small-Cap: The innovative startup garages and workshops on the edge of town, where the next big thing might be born (Russell 2000).

Sector Indexes (The Themed Quarters): Want to explore a specific part of the economy? There's a neighborhood for that. You can visit the Financial District, the Healthcare and Biotech hub, or the Energy quarter, each with its own dedicated index.

Global Indexes (The World Tour): These indexes are your passport to investing around the world. The MSCI World Index takes you on a tour of developed countries, while the MSCI Emerging Markets Index is your guide to the fast-growing economies of tomorrow.

Dividend Indexes (The Landlord's Lane): This is a tour of the companies that are masters of sharing the wealth. The S&P 500 Dividend Aristocrats index, for example, only includes companies that have reliably increased their dividend payouts to shareholders for at least 25 straight years. 🤑

ESG Indexes (The Green Zone): A newer, but increasingly popular tour, these indexes guide you to the city's most sustainable and socially responsible neighborhoods. They include companies that score high on Environmental, Social, and Governance metrics, letting you invest with your values.

1. The Market's Personality Test: Decoding Stock Indexes

Think of a stock market index not as a boring graph, but as a personality test for the entire economy. It's a snapshot that tries to answer the question, "So, how are things really going?" But just like a personality test, the answer you get depends entirely on the questions you ask and who you ask them to. The way an index is built reveals what it truly values, and that can make all the difference.

Imagine you walk into a room to gauge its mood. Whose opinion do you trust? This is the core of index weighting.

The Price-Weighted Index is like listening to the loudest person in the room. The Dow Jones Industrial Average (DJIA) is this person. In this world, a stock's influence is based purely on its price tag per share. A company with a $500 stock price gets five times the say of a company with a $100 stock price, even if the $100 company is a global behemoth and the $500 one is a niche player. It's a simple, old-school method, but it can feel a bit like giving the most attention to someone just because they have the highest-pitched voice, not because they have the most important thing to say.

The Value-Weighted Index, on the other hand, is like listening to the person with the most skin in the game. This is the world of the S&P 500. Here, influence is determined by a company's total market value (its stock price multiplied by all its shares). In this room, giants like Apple and Microsoft don't just speak; their voices boom, while smaller companies whisper. This method argues that a company's economic footprint—its sheer size—is what matters. If a company takes up a huge slice of the economic pie, its ups and downs should logically create the biggest ripples.

Then there's the Equally-Weighted Index, the true democracy of the market. In this room, every single company gets one vote, regardless of its price or size. A tiny tech startup has the exact same pull as a multinational conglomerate. To keep this perfect balance, the index is constantly playing Robin Hood—selling off a little bit of the winners who have grown too influential and buying a bit more of the underdogs. It can be a costlier strategy, but it gives you a powerful, unfiltered look at how the "average" stock is doing, free from the shadow of the market's mega-celebrities.

Beyond this popularity contest, indexes slice and dice the market in endless ways. There are indexes for the whole shebang (like the Wilshire 5000), and there are exclusive clubs for just tech, healthcare, or energy stocks. They can zoom in on small, scrappy companies or focus on global titans. Each one is a unique lens, a different story about a pocket of the financial universe, waiting to be read.

2. The Pulse of IOUs: A Guide to Bond Indexes

If stock indexes are the market's personality test, then fixed-income indexes are its heartbeat monitor. They track the world of bonds—the universe of IOUs—from the ultra-safe to the daringly risky. They don't measure the explosive dreams of future growth; they measure the steady, rhythmic pulse of debt, income, and interest rates. Understanding them is like learning to read an EKG, revealing the underlying health and stress levels of economies and corporations.

At the center of it all are Government Bond Indexes. Think of these as tracking the credit of the most reliable entity in the country, like Uncle Sam. These indexes, which follow Treasury bills and bonds, are the benchmark for safety. They don't worry about a company going bankrupt; they worry about interest rates. When the Federal Reserve tweaks interest rates, these bonds feel it first and most directly. Their performance is the baseline, the "risk-free" rhythm against which all other, riskier heartbeats are measured.

Next are Corporate Bond Indexes, which monitor the IOUs of the business world. This is where things get interesting, because not all companies are created equal. Investment-Grade Indexes are like the EKG of large, healthy, blue-chip corporations. These are the reliable, steady businesses that are very likely to pay you back. They offer a slightly higher return (yield) than government bonds as a little thank-you for trusting them. Their pulse is steady, influenced by both interest rates and the general health of the economy.

Then you have the High-Yield "Junk" Bond Indexes. This is the adrenaline-fueled EKG of the corporate world. These indexes track the debt of companies that are on shakier ground—startups, companies in turnarounds, or those in volatile industries. The risk of default is real, but the potential reward is much higher. These bonds are the thrill-seekers of the fixed-income world, and their performance often feels more like the wild ride of the stock market. Their heartbeat can get dangerously erratic during an economic downturn.

Just as a doctor might listen to a heartbeat over seconds or minutes, bond indexes are also segmented by time, or Maturity. Short-term indexes track loans that will be paid back soon, making them relatively stable and less sensitive to interest rate mood swings. Long-term indexes, tracking debt that won't be paid back for a decade or more, are a different story. They are like a long, sensitive lever—a tiny change in interest rates today can cause a huge swing in their value.

From here, the world gets even more specific, with indexes for tax-free municipal bonds that fund our schools and roads, or mortgage-backed securities that track the rhythm of the nation's housing payments. Each one tells a unique story of debt and obligation, a vital pulse in the complex anatomy of our financial system.

3. Mapping the Uncharted: Indexes for Alternative Investments

Welcome to the wild frontier of finance. Alternative investments are the assets that don't fit neatly into the boxes of "stocks" or "bonds." They are the real estate we walk on, the commodities we consume, and the secret strategies of financial wizards. Trying to create an index for these things is like trying to map an uncharted jungle—it's complex, the terrain is uneven, and the landmarks are constantly shifting. But these maps, however imperfect, are our best guide to these mysterious and often lucrative worlds.

One of the most tangible frontiers is Real Estate. While you can't exactly track the daily value of every brick and window in a city, you can track REITs (Real Estate Investment Trusts). These are companies that own and operate vast portfolios of buildings—malls, apartment complexes, office towers—and trade on the stock exchange. REIT indexes, therefore, act as our proxy, our satellite view of the property market. They give us a liquid, real-time signal of the health of the ground beneath our feet, influenced by everything from interest rates to the national trend of working from home.

Next, we map the planet's pantry with Commodity Indexes. These indexes track the raw ingredients of civilization: the price of oil that fuels our cars, the gold that backs our currencies, the wheat that becomes our bread. They don't follow corporate earnings; they follow the raw, primal forces of supply and demand, of droughts and discoveries, of geopolitical tensions and technological breakthroughs. They are a barometer of global inflation and industrial hunger, offering a gritty, real-world diversification from the more abstract world of corporate finance.

Perhaps the most mysterious territory is the one tracked by Hedge Fund Indexes. This is an attempt to map the performance of the world's most secretive and sophisticated investors. The challenge is immense. Hedge funds are private, their strategies are complex, and they report their performance voluntarily. This creates a "fog of war" for index makers. They battle biases like survivorship bias, where the score is artificially inflated because all the failed funds disappear from the records. It's like judging a singing competition by only listening to the finalists, never the ones who were booed off stage. These indexes are imperfect windows, but they are often the only windows we have into this high-stakes world.

Finally, we venture into the realms of Private Equity and Infrastructure. These indexes try to measure the value of things that are almost never for sale: private companies being nurtured for years before a potential public debut, or massive infrastructure projects like toll roads and airports. Creating a real-time index here is nearly impossible. Instead, these maps are drawn from appraisals, complex models, and data that can be months old. They are slow-moving, lagging indicators, but they represent the patient, long-term bets being made on the foundational, often invisible, pillars of our economy. Each of these alternative maps opens our eyes to a different dimension of value, proving that in the world of investment, there is always more territory to explore.

Market Efficiency

Imagine the stock market as a colossal, hyper-caffeinated brain, constantly processing every tidbit of information the world throws at it. Every news flash, every earnings report, every political tremor, every whisper of a rumor. The theory of market efficiency is the bold claim that this giant brain works so fast that the prices you see on your screen already reflect everything that is known. It's a concept that doesn't just live in textbooks; it's the ghost in the machine that shapes every investment decision, from the pension fund manager handling billions to you checking a stock on your phone.

If this idea is true, then trying to consistently "beat the market" is like trying to outrun your own shadow. It's always one step ahead. This powerful notion forces every investor to ask a fundamental question: Am I a believer or a challenger? Your answer dictates your entire financial strategy.

The Supporting Cast of a Grand Theory

Market efficiency doesn't stand alone; it's propped up by a fascinating cast of related ideas.

First, meet the random walk theory, which paints a picture of stock prices moving like a tipsy wanderer stumbling home from the pub. His next step is completely unpredictable. Why? Because if the market is efficient, prices only move in response to new, unexpected information. And if the information is truly new, by definition, you can't predict it. Following past price charts, in this view, is like trying to predict the wanderer's path by looking at his footprints in the snow—they only tell you where he's been, not where he's going.

Then there's the specter of information asymmetry. Picture a card game where one player gets a peek at everyone else's hand. That's information asymmetry. In a perfectly efficient market, this couldn't happen; everyone would see all the cards at the same time. In reality, though, these informational advantages exist, creating brief, shadowy opportunities for those "in the know" to profit before the light of public knowledge floods the room.

The active enforcer of efficiency is the arbitrage principle. Think of arbitrageurs as the market's hyper-vigilant price police. The moment a stock is selling for $10 in New York and $10.05 in London, they swoop in, buying low and selling high in a flurry of activity that slams the prices back into alignment. Their relentless, self-interested pursuit of these risk-free profits is precisely what irons out the market's wrinkles, making it a smoother, more efficient fabric.

The Soul of a Stock: Market Value vs. Intrinsic Value

At the heart of the investment debate is a tale of two values: the popular, flashy market value and the thoughtful, elusive intrinsic value.

Market Value is the price tag you see right now. It's the popular kid at the party, swayed by gossip, excitement, and momentary panic. It's the number on the ticker, a real-time poll of the collective mood of millions of investors. It's objective, it's loud, and it's what a share is "worth" in this very second.

Intrinsic Value is its soul. It's the value an asset should have, based on its true, underlying ability to generate cash and grow over time. It's an estimate, a piece of art painted with the brushstrokes of discounted cash flow models (DCF) and deep financial analysis. It ignores the market's party noise and tries to understand the asset's deep character. Calculating it is an attempt to answer the question: "If I owned this entire business, what would it truly be worth to me over the long haul?"

The entire game of value investing, championed by legends like Warren Buffett, is built on the gap between these two. A value investor is like a treasure hunter, patiently sifting through the market's noisy bazaar, looking for beautiful assets that are temporarily unpopular—where the market value has fallen far below the intrinsic value. They buy this "hidden gem" and wait, confident that, in the long run, the crowd will eventually recognize its true worth, and the price tag will rise to meet its soul. This requires an almost zen-like patience, a belief that substance will ultimately triumph over sentiment.

What Makes a Market Smart? The Ingredients of Efficiency

A market's "IQ" isn't fixed; it's a spectrum. Several key ingredients determine whether a market is a razor-sharp supercomputer or a sluggish, forgetful machine.

The Crowd: A market with millions of savvy, professional, and diverse investors is like a kitchen with countless expert chefs. Any bad ingredient (a mispriced stock) is spotted and corrected instantly. A small market with few, unsophisticated participants is more likely to let things burn.

Sunlight and Megaphones: Information is the lifeblood. Markets thrive on transparency—clear financial reporting, widespread news, and equal access. When information flows freely like sunlight, it disinfects bad ideas and poor valuations. Secrecy and insider knowledge are the enemies of efficiency.

Friction and Sludge: Transaction costs—like fees and taxes—are the sludge in the market's gears. If it costs too much to make a trade, investors might not bother correcting a small mispricing, allowing the inefficiency to persist. The modern era of low-cost trading has been like a power wash for these gears.

The Ghost in the Machine: This is us. Human psychology. We are not the perfectly rational beings the classic theory assumes. We fall prey to herd mentality, panic selling, and irrational exuberance. These behavioral biases are the ghosts that haunt the market, creating bubbles and crashes that defy cold logic and create massive, terrifying inefficiencies.

The Supercharger: Technology has put a rocket booster on efficiency. High-frequency trading algorithms can read a news report and execute a million trades before a human has even finished the headline. Information now travels at the speed of light, and the market reacts almost as quickly.

The Three Levels of Market Wisdom

The Efficient Market Hypothesis (EMH) isn't a single belief but a staircase of three ascending levels of faith.

Level 1: The Weak Form

This is the ground floor. It claims that all past price and volume data is already baked into today's price. This makes technical analysis—the art of reading charts to find patterns—a fool's errand. The market, in this view, has amnesia; it doesn't remember its past movements, so you can't use them to predict its future. Driving by looking only in the rearview mirror is a recipe for disaster.

Level 2: The Semi-Strong Form
Take a step up. This form argues that the market is the world's fastest gossip. It instantly absorbs all publicly available information. By the time you read a company's glowing earnings report or see a news flash about a merger, the price has already adjusted. The profit opportunity has vanished. This suggests that even fundamental analysis based on public data is a tough way to get an edge, pushing many to simply buy the whole market through an index fund.

Level 3: The Strong Form
This is the top floor, a theoretical utopia. It posits that prices reflect all information, both public and private. This means even the secret knowledge held by a CEO is somehow, mystically, already in the stock price. If this were true, insider trading would be impossible. Of course, the very existence of laws against insider trading is the strongest evidence that we don't live in this perfect world. This form remains a beautiful, but largely unattainable, ideal.

For any investment practitioner, this journey through market efficiency isn't just an academic exercise. It's a search for a personal philosophy. Are you a passive believer, content to ride the market's wave? Or are you an active challenger, dedicating your resources to hunting for the inefficiencies, the gaps between price and soul, that our messy, human, and endlessly fascinating markets will always create? The answer defines not just how you invest, but how you see the world.

The financial market is often spoken of as a single, colossal entity—a machine that crunches data and spits out prices. But what if we thought of it differently? What if we saw it not as a machine, but as a vast, global conversation? A roaring, chaotic, and sometimes whispered exchange of hopes, fears, and calculations.

At the heart of this conversation is a single, driving question: What is something worth? The quest to answer this leads us to the idea of market efficiency—a theory about how well the market's "conversation" incorporates information. But just as any human conversation is prone to gossip, stubbornness, and wild emotion, the market, too, has its quirks. These are the fascinating glitches and psychological tics that make investing less a science and more a study of human nature itself.

The Tale of Three Mirrors: How Much Does the Market Really Know?

The Efficient Market Hypothesis (EMH) is a powerful idea that suggests the market is a master of information. It comes in three flavors, each painting a different picture of the market's omniscience, like looking into three different mirrors.

1. The Rearview Mirror (Weak-Form Efficiency)

Imagine driving a car where the rearview mirror is perfectly clear, showing you every inch of the road you've already traveled. This is a weak-form efficient market. It suggests that all past price movements and trading volumes are already baked into today's stock price.

For the Chart-Gazer (Technical Analyst): This mirror makes your job impossible. You study historical charts for clues about the future, but if this theory holds, you're just staring at old news. All the squiggles, patterns, and trends are already reflected in the current price. It's like trying to predict where you're going by only looking at the road behind you.

For the Detective (Fundamental Analyst): You, however, still have a job. You're not looking in the rearview mirror; you're looking out the windshield and under the hood. You analyze a company's health, its leadership, and its place in the world to find its "true" value. The market may know its own past, but you believe it might have missed a crucial detail about the future.

For the Everyday Investor (Active vs. Passive): This world suggests that trying to "time the market" based on past performance is a fool's errand. A passive strategy, like buying an index fund that simply mirrors the market, starts to look pretty smart. Why pay an active manager to stare at charts when the information is already priced in?

2. The Glass House (Semi-Strong Form Efficiency)

Now, imagine the market is a house made entirely of glass. Not only can you see the past, but you can see everything happening right now, in public view. All the company reports, news headlines, and expert analyses are instantly visible to everyone and absorbed into the stock prices.

For the Detective (Fundamental Analyst): Your job just became incredibly difficult. Every clue you uncover from public records—a company's quarterly earnings, a new product announcement—is already part of the house's transparent architecture. To find an edge, you can't just find the information; you have to understand it better and faster than millions of others who are staring at the exact same thing.

For the Chart-Gazer (Technical Analyst): You're still out of luck. Your rearview mirror is now just a small part of a much bigger, all-encompassing view that everyone already shares.

For the Everyday Investor (Active vs. Passive): The case for going passive becomes almost overwhelming. If professional detectives with powerful computers can't find an edge in this glass house, what chance does the average person have? The goal shifts from "beating the market" to simply "being the market" through low-cost index funds. It's a humble but powerful admission that the collective wisdom of the crowd is too hard to outsmart.

3. The All-Seeing Eye (Strong-Form Efficiency)

This is the most extreme, almost mythical, version of efficiency. The market is no longer a glass house; it's a psychic. It knows everything—public news, private secrets, the whispers in the boardroom, the plans on the CEO's laptop. All information, even illegal insider knowledge, is instantly and perfectly reflected in the stock price.

For Everyone (Analysts and Investors): In this world, the game is over before it begins. There are no secrets, no hidden gems, no advantages to be had. Any attempt at active management is an exercise in futility and fees.

The Only Move Left: The only logical choice is to be a passive investor. You accept that you cannot outsmart an all-knowing entity. Your focus becomes building a diversified portfolio that captures the market's overall return, managing your risk, and minimizing costs.

Ghosts in the Machine: The Market's Mysterious Quirks

If markets were perfectly efficient, they would be predictable and, frankly, a little boring. But they aren't. Academics and investors have found persistent "anomalies"—ghosts in the machine that defy the cold logic of efficiency.

The David vs. Goliath Glitch (Size Effect): For decades, the little guys (small-cap stocks) have often outperformed the Goliaths (large-cap stocks), even when adjusting for risk. It's a puzzle: why should being smaller consistently lead to better returns?

The Wallflower's Revenge (Value Effect): Stocks that look "cheap" or "boring" based on metrics like a low price-to-earnings ratio (P/E) have a history of outperforming their glamorous, high-growth counterparts. It's as if the market consistently overlooks the quiet wallflowers at the dance, only to see them shine brightest in the long run.

The Hot Hand (Momentum Anomaly): A stock that's been winning tends to keep winning for the next few months, and losers tend to keep losing. This flies in the face of efficiency, which says each day is a new day and past performance is irrelevant. It's as if the market, like a basketball player on a streak, develops a "hot hand."

The New Year's Resolution Rally (January Effect): Historically, stocks, especially small ones, get a shot of adrenaline in January. The common explanation is a year-end "tax-loss harvesting" sale in December, followed by a new-year buying spree.

The Slow News Day (Earnings Announcement Drift): When a company posts a surprise—good or bad—the stock price doesn't just jump and settle. It often continues to drift in the direction of the surprise for weeks. It's as if the market is a slow reader, taking its time to fully digest the news.

The Market's Mood Swings (Weekend & Holiday Effects): The market seems to get the "Monday Blues," with historically lower returns. Conversely, it gets a bit of

"Holiday Cheer," with returns often being higher on the day before a public holiday.

The Human Factor: The Heartbeat Driving the Machine

So why do these ghosts exist? Why isn't the market a perfectly logical machine? The answer is simple and profound: because we aren't. Behavioral finance pulls back the curtain on the EMH to reveal that the market isn't driven by robots, but by a global collective of humans, with all our brilliant, messy, and irrational psychology.

These anomalies are not glitches in a machine; they are the fingerprints of human nature.

The Bugs in Our Mental Software (Cognitive Biases):

The Echo Chamber (Confirmation Bias): We crave proof that we're right. We hunt for news that validates our decision to buy a stock and subconsciously ignore the warning signs.

The "I Am a Genius" Trap (Overconfidence): After a few winning trades, we don't thank luck; we thank our own brilliance. This leads to excessive trading and taking on foolish risks.

Stuck on a Price Tag (Anchoring): We get psychologically tethered to a number, like the price we paid for a stock. We hold on to a loser, praying it will return to our "anchor" price, even as its fundamentals crumble.

The Heart Hijacking the Head (Emotional Biases):

The Agony of Defeat (Loss Aversion): Psychologically, the pain of losing $100 feels twice as intense as the joy of gaining $100. This makes us sell our winners too early to lock in a small pleasure, and hold our losers far too long to avoid the pain of realizing a loss.

Fear of Missing Out (Herding): When we see the crowd rushing toward a hot stock, our instinct isn't to ask why, but to run along with them. This herd mentality is what inflates bubbles and what turns downturns into panics.

These human impulses offer compelling explanations for the market's ghosts. The Momentum Anomaly is the signature of a slow-burn reaction followed by a herding stampede. The Value Effect exists because investors, blinded by overconfidence and the allure of exciting stories, overpay for growth and neglect solid, unglamorous companies. Asset bubbles and crashes are the ultimate monuments to collective greed and fear.

In the end, the financial market is one of humanity's most complex creations. It strives for efficiency, constantly digesting information in a relentless pursuit of value. But it is, and always will be, a system powered by people. It is a mirror that reflects not just data and balance sheets, but our own collective psychology—our brilliance, our biases, our moments of genius, and our episodes of madness. And understanding that human element is the ultimate key to navigating its intricate dance.

Overview of Equity Securities

The Investor's Compass: Navigating the World of Equity

Think of owning a piece of a company not as holding a dry certificate, but as joining the crew of a ship on a grand voyage. Each share is your ticket aboard, your stake in the journey. Some voyages are on well-known cruise liners, others on nimble private yachts, and some are expeditions to foreign shores. Your experience—the risks you take, the rewards you reap, and the say you have in the ship's direction—all depends on the type of ticket you hold.

1. Choosing Your Role: The Crew, the VIPs, and the Map-Holders

When you buy into a company, you're not just a number on a ledger; you're choosing your role on the vessel.

The most common ticket makes you part of the Common Stock crew. You are the lifeblood of the ship. This ticket grants you a voice at the captain's table—you get voting rights. You help elect the board of directors, the seasoned officers who steer the company. You vote on major decisions, like whether to merge fleets with another company or change the ship's charter. In return for your work and your risk, you get a share of the treasure found along the way, whether through a rising stock price or a cut of the profits called dividends. But being part of the crew comes with a catch: you have a "residual claim." If the ship sinks in a storm of bankruptcy, you're the last to the lifeboats, paid only after everyone else is safe. The risk is high, but the potential reward—a share in a legendary treasure—is unlimited.

Then there's the Preferred Stock ticket, which is more like being a first-class passenger. You pay your fare and get to enjoy a smoother, more predictable journey. You have no say in navigating the ship—no voting rights—but you're served your meals first. This comes in the form of a fixed dividend, a predictable payment that must be made to you before the common crew gets their share. If the company misses a dividend payment, it owes you back pay before the crew sees a single gold coin. And if the ship goes down, you have priority access to the lifeboats over the common stockholders. You trade the thrill of discovery and the potential for immense riches for comfort, security, and a steady income.

Beyond the crew and passengers, there are the Warrants. Think of these not as a ticket for this voyage, but as a treasure map with a special clause. A warrant gives you the right to buy a ticket (a share of stock) for a pre-set price at a later date. It's often given as a sweetener to those who lend the ship money. If the ship discovers a legendary island of riches and the value of its voyage skyrockets, your map becomes incredibly valuable, allowing you to join the expedition at the old, cheaper price.

Finally, how do you join the voyage of a ship from a foreign land? You use a Depositary Receipt (DR). This is like booking an exotic expedition through a trusted local travel agent. The agent (a bank) holds the foreign ticket for you and gives you a simple certificate, an American Depositary Receipt (ADR), that you can trade easily in your own country and your own currency. It lets you experience the thrill of a global journey without the headache of converting currency or navigating the strange customs of a foreign port.

2. The Politics of the Ship: Voice, Power, and Control

The difference between these roles isn't just about money; it's about power.

As a common stockholder, your vote is your voice. It's the democratic heart of the corporation. But sometimes, not all voices are equal. Imagine a ship where the founding family wants to maintain control of the helm. They might create different classes of crew tickets. Class A shares might get one vote each, while the family holds Class B shares that carry ten votes each. This allows them to guide the ship according to their vision, even if they no longer own more than half of it. It's a reminder that even among the crew, there can be an inner circle with more say in the ship's destiny.

Preferred stockholders, by contrast, are silent partners. They have traded their voice for privilege. Their relationship with the company is built on a contract of priority, not a partnership of equals. They are lenders in spirit, owners in name, content to watch the voyage unfold from their comfortable cabins as long as their dividends arrive on schedule.

3. Public Oceans vs. Private Lagoons

Equity voyages can happen in two very different environments: the vast, open ocean of public markets or the secluded, uncharted lagoons of private equity.

Public Equity is the grand cruise liner listed on a stock exchange. Anyone can buy a ticket. Its journey is tracked on public maps, and its logs—its financial reports—are open for all to inspect, thanks to strict regulations from bodies like the Securities and Exchange Commission (SEC). This transparency and the ability to hop on or off the ship at any public port (high liquidity) is its greatest strength. But this openness also means the ship is subject to the constant tides of market sentiment and public opinion, making for a potentially volatile ride.

Private Equity, however, is an exclusive expedition on a private vessel. The shares aren't traded in a public harbor; they are held by a select few—venture capitalists, founders, and specialized firms. To get aboard, you need an invitation and deep pockets. The journey is long, and you can't simply disembark whenever you please; selling your stake is a complex, negotiated process (it's illiquid). The ship's logs are kept private, free from the prying eyes of the public and subject to far less regulation. The risks are higher, and the waters are uncharted, but the potential discoveries can be world-changing, offering returns that are often impossible to find on the open ocean.

4. Charting a Course for Global Markets

To truly diversify your fleet, you must look beyond your home waters. Investing in non-domestic companies is like becoming a global explorer, and there are several ways to chart your course.

The Direct Expedition: The bravest method is direct investment. You learn the local customs, navigate foreign exchanges, and deal with currency fluctuations yourself. It's a hands-on approach that offers total control but is fraught with complexity, best suited for the most seasoned global navigators.

The Guided Tour: A far more popular method is to invest through international ETFs or Mutual Funds. This is like joining a professionally managed fleet. Instead of betting on a single ship, you own a small piece of an entire armada sailing in European, Asian, or emerging market waters. The fund manager handles all the navigation and currency conversions, giving you instant diversification and peace of mind.

The Local Agent: As we've seen, Depositary Receipts (ADRs) are your trusted travel agent, "localizing" a foreign investment. You can buy a piece of a German automaker or a Japanese tech giant right from your U.S. brokerage account, in U.S. dollars. It's the simplest way to own a direct piece of a foreign enterprise.

The Global Harbor: Finally, you can invest in multinational corporations based in your own country. Buying shares in a company like Apple or Coca-Cola is like investing in a massive, home-based shipping company whose fleet does business in every corner of the world. While the company is domestic, its fortunes are tied to the health of the global economy, giving you indirect international exposure from the comfort of your home port.

1. The Investor's Menu: Choosing Your Stock Market Flavor

Think of the stock market as a massive, bustling food court, with every company offering a different dish. Each one promises a unique flavor (return) but comes with its own level of spice (risk). Your job as an investor is to build a meal that satisfies your appetite without giving you heartburn.

Common Stock: The Ghost Pepper Challenge

This is the dish for the thrill-seeker, the one who wants a story to tell. Ordering common stock is like saying, "Hit me with your best shot." You're not just a customer; you're a part-owner of the restaurant. You get a vote on the decor and the new specials. If the chef becomes a global sensation, your meal ticket could be worth a fortune (capital appreciation). The chef might even share some of the profits with you (dividends). But be warned: if the restaurant goes under, the suppliers, the landlords, and everyone else get paid before you see a single dime. You might be left with nothing but a memory and a scorched palate. It's the ultimate high-risk, high-reward culinary adventure.

Preferred Stock: The Comfort Food Classic

This is the reliable mac and cheese of the investment world. Preferred stock is for those who crave predictability. You won't get a vote on the menu, but you're promised a consistent, fixed portion of flavor (dividends) delivered to your table before the common stock folks even get their water. It's less volatile, less dramatic. In a downturn, it feels safe and warm. But don't expect it to change your life. It's a satisfying meal, but it's not designed to be a mind-blowing gastronomic event. You trade the potential for wild, explosive gains for the peace of mind that comes with a steady, comforting dish.

Convertible Securities: The "Surf and Turf" Special

Can't decide between the steady comfort of a steak and the exciting potential of lobster? Convertible securities let you have both. You start with the reliable, dividend-paying nature of a preferred stock—the "steak." But tucked in your pocket is a magic fork that lets you transform your meal into a heaping portion of common stock—the "lobster"—if you see that the chef is about to win a Michelin star. It's the ultimate "what if" option. You get the safety net of a predictable meal with a lottery ticket for something spectacular. This is for the investor who wants a taste of security but suffers from a serious case of FOMO (Fear Of Missing Out) on the upside.

A La Carte: Blue-Chips, Growth, and Value

Blue-Chip Stocks: This is the world-famous chain restaurant you can find in any city. Think Coca-Cola or Apple. The recipe is proven, the quality is consistent, and you know exactly what you're getting. It's not the most exciting meal of your life, but it's dependable and will always leave you satisfied.

Growth Stocks: This is the trendy new fusion food truck with a line around the block. The hype is real, and the flavors could be revolutionary. Everyone is betting this truck will become the next big thing. You won't get any leftovers (dividends) because all profits are used to buy a bigger truck. The risk? It could just be a fad that's gone by next season.

Value Stocks: This is the hidden gem—the shabby-looking diner that the locals swear by. The critics ignore it, and its decor is twenty years out of date. But inside, they serve the best burger in town for half the price of anywhere else. You're betting that one day, a famous food critic will wander in and tell the world, sending its value skyrocketing. The risk is that it remains a well-kept secret forever.

2. Building the Dream: How Equity Forges a Company's Destiny

Imagine a company isn't just a business, but a grand ship destined for uncharted waters. How do you build such a vessel? You can't just borrow some logs; you need a foundation. That's where equity comes in.

Equity is the very soul of the ship. It's the blueprint drawn from a founder's dream, funded by early believers—angel investors and venture capitalists—who provide the cash to lay the keel and raise the first mast. This isn't a loan to be repaid; it's a shared dream. These initial investors become part-owners of the vessel, betting that the voyage will be a legendary one. Without this first act of faith, the ship would never be more than a drawing on a napkin.

As the ship proves its worth on coastal voyages, the time comes for a grander ambition: crossing the ocean. To do this, it needs to be bigger, stronger, and outfitted with the best technology—new factories, groundbreaking research, and a larger crew. This is where the shipwright (the company) might invite the public to become co-owners through an IPO. Everyday people can buy a piece of the ship, and their investment provides the steel, timber, and canvas to transform a humble vessel into a majestic galleon. This infusion of cash isn't a debt hanging over the captain's head. It's permanent capital, woven into the very fabric of the ship, making it more resilient for the long, uncertain journey ahead.

This is equity's greatest magic: it provides buoyancy. A ship financed heavily by debt is like a vessel overloaded with cargo it has promised to deliver by a specific date. The slightest storm or a delay in the winds can send it to the bottom, crushed by its obligations. A ship built with a strong hull of equity, however, can weather the fiercest tempests. If profits dip, there are no angry lenders demanding their payments. The ship simply sails on, supported by the capital of its co-owners who are in it for the long haul.

This resilience gives the captain the courage to steer toward the "X" on the map—the risky, long-term ventures like developing a revolutionary product or exploring a new market. You can't finance a quest for a new world with a loan due next Tuesday. Equity provides the patient capital, the fuel for a journey whose rewards may be years away.

Ultimately, a ship with a strong, solid hull inspires confidence. Lenders are far more willing to offer supplies (debt) on favorable terms to a vessel they know is seaworthy. A robust equity base doesn't just fund the dream; it makes the entire journey safer, cheaper, and more likely to succeed. It is, and always will be, the core strength that allows a company to set sail and chase the horizon.

3. The Resume vs. The Reputation: A Tale of Two Values

When trying to understand a person, you might look at two things: their resume and their reputation. A company's value works the same way. We have its book value (the resume) and its market value (the reputation). They tell two very different, though equally important, stories.

Book Value: The Official Resume

The book value is a company's life story told by an accountant. It's a cold, hard list of everything the company owns (assets) minus everything it owes (liabilities). It's printed on the balance sheet, following strict rules. Think of it as a resume: "Graduated with a degree in Engineering (cost: $100k). Acquired machinery (cost: $500k). Built a factory (cost: $1M)." It's historical, factual, and backward-looking. It tells you the net cost of everything that has been invested into the company to date. It's the tangible, verifiable paper trail of what the company is "made of," according to the books.

Market Value: The Street Reputation

The market value is the company's living, breathing reputation. It's the buzz, the gossip, the collective feeling of millions of people in the public square (the stock market). Calculated by multiplying the current stock price by the number of shares, it has almost nothing to do with historical cost and everything to do with future promise. It's the answer to the question, "What do we think this company is going to do next?"

This reputation accounts for all the things that can't be put on a resume: the genius and charisma of its leader, the secret recipe that no one can copy, the fierce loyalty of its customers, and the feeling that it's on the cusp of changing the world. It's dynamic, emotional, and can change in a heartbeat based on a single rumor or a grand vision.

Where the Stories Diverge

Here's the fascinating part. A hotshot tech startup might have a resume that's almost blank (a tiny book value), but its reputation is electric (a massive market value). The world isn't betting on its past; it's betting on its brilliant future.

Conversely, an old, established manufacturing giant might have a long and impressive resume filled with valuable factories and equipment (a huge book value). But its reputation might be fading. The market might see it as a dinosaur, whispering that its best days are behind it (a market value lower than its book value).

Investors live and breathe reputation because it reflects future potential. But the resume provides a crucial reality check. It grounds the conversation, offering a baseline of tangible worth. One tells you what it cost to build the machine; the other tells you what people believe that machine can do tomorrow. To truly know a company, you must read both.

4. The Trainer, The Client, and The Gym: A Performance Triangle

Imagine a company is a personal trainer. Its ultimate job is to take the resources it's given and produce amazing results. To understand if it's succeeding, we need to listen in on a three-way conversation between the company's performance, its investors' goals, and its own internal standards.

1. The Return on Equity (ROE): The Actual Workout Result

This is the trainer's bottom-line performance. It's the answer to the question, "What did you actually accomplish with the money my shareholders gave you?" It's a historical fact, like a reading on a heart rate monitor after a workout. Calculated as Net Income divided by Shareholder Equity, an ROE of 15% means the trainer took every $100 of client investment and turned it into $15 of pure fitness gains (profit). It's the proof of what the company has done.

2. The Cost of Equity: The Gym's Minimum Standard

This is the official benchmark set by the "gym" (the financial market). It's the minimum performance level the trainer must achieve to be considered competent and to justify their fees. It's a forward-looking hurdle rate that says, "Given the difficulty of this workout (risk), you must generate at least a 12% return, or we'll find a new trainer." This standard is influenced by how risky the workout is (a company's volatility) and what other gyms are offering. It's the bar the company must clear to create value.

3. The Investor's Required Rate of Return: The Client's Personal Goal

This is the most personal piece of the puzzle. It's the client (the investor) sitting down with the trainer and saying, "Look, I have a wedding in six months, and I've seen other trainers getting amazing results. To make this worth my time and money, I need you to deliver a 14% return. If you can't promise that, I'm walking." This required return is unique to each investor. It's their personal ambition, shaped by their own goals, their tolerance for pain (risk), and the other trainers they could hire (alternative investments).

The Moment of Truth

The magic happens when you compare these three numbers.

A great company is a star trainer whose workout results (ROE) consistently blast past both the gym's minimum standards (Cost of Equity) and the client's personal goals (Required Rate of Return). When ROE > Cost of Equity, the trainer is not just meeting expectations; they are actively creating value, making the client stronger and more successful. The client is thrilled and tells everyone about their amazing trainer, driving up their reputation (stock price).

A struggling company is a trainer whose results (ROE) fall short of the gym's minimum (Cost of Equity). Even if the client is seeing some progress, the trainer is fundamentally failing. They are destroying value because they can't even clear the minimum bar required for their risk level. Sooner or later, the client will realize they can get better results elsewhere and will fire the trainer, sending their reputation plummeting.

Company Analysis: Past and Present

The Art of Seeing a Company: A Guide for the Curious Mind

Getting to know a company is like getting to know a person. On the surface, you see what they do for a living. But to truly understand them, you have to dig deeper—into their history, their character, their relationships, and how they handle money and stress. It's not about crunching numbers in a vacuum; it's about piecing together a story. Let's explore how to become a corporate biographer, decoding the very soul of a business.

Part 1: Crafting the Company Portrait

A great research report is a portrait, not a photograph. It captures the essence, the personality, and the hidden details that tell the real story.

The Movie Trailer (Executive Summary): Before anyone commits to the full feature film, they watch the trailer. This is it. In two minutes, give them the explosions, the drama, and the profound conclusion. It's the entire story—the good, the bad, and your final verdict—distilled into a potent, can't-miss summary.

The Birth Certificate & Persona (Company Description): Every story needs a protagonist. Who is this company? Let's get its origin story. Where was it born? What's its mission—the noble quest it claims to be on? What are its core values? This is where you introduce the character, its size, and the ground it stands on.

The Neighborhood & The Rivals (Industry & Competitive Analysis): No one lives on a deserted island. What neighborhood does this company live in? Is it a booming, gentrifying metropolis or a forgotten, dusty town? Who are the other big players on the block? You need to size them up—the schoolyard bully, the scrappy upstart, the wise old veteran. This is about understanding the "sandbox" the company plays in and how it carves out its own corner to build its castle. What's its moat? What unique advantage keeps the rivals at bay?

Meet the Captains of the Ship (Management & Governance): A ship is only as good as the captain and crew steering it through storms. Who is at the helm? Look the leadership team in the eye (metaphorically). Are they seasoned sailors with a map of the stars, or are they reckless pirates? A strong, independent board of directors acts as the steadying hand on the tiller, ensuring the ship isn't steered toward the rocks. The culture they foster is the wind in the sails.

The X-Ray Vision (Financial Analysis): Now, we put on our x-ray goggles. It's time to look past the skin and see the bones. The financial statements—income statement, balance sheet, cash flow—are the company's medical charts. We're not just looking at a single snapshot; we're tracking its health over time. Is its heartbeat (profit) steady? Is its skeleton (assets vs. liabilities) strong? Is its circulation (cash flow) healthy? Ratios are our diagnostic tools, telling us if the company is fit, running on fumes, or dangerously over-leveraged. This reveals the unvarnished truth of its physical condition.

Reading the Tea Leaves (Future Outlook): Based on everything we've learned, where is this story going? What are the next chapters? We look at the company's own plans—new products, new markets, new adventures. We also look at the external world. Are there tailwinds like a new technology or cultural shift that will push it forward?

Or are there headwinds like a looming recession or new regulations that threaten to blow it off course?

The Dragons in the Dungeon (Key Risks): Every protagonist has a weakness, every castle a hidden dragon. What are the things that keep the CEO up at night? Fierce competition? A reliance on a single supplier? The threat of being made obsolete? More importantly, what is their plan to slay these dragons? A company that understands its own vulnerabilities and has a plan to defend them is far stronger than one that pretends they don't exist.

The Evidence Locker (Appendix & Sources): Every good detective shows their work. This is your evidence locker—the charts, the data, and the sources that back up your story. It builds trust and lets others follow your trail of discovery.

Part 2: Decoding the DNA—The Business Model

A business model is a company's secret sauce. It's the unique recipe for how it creates something people want, gets it into their hands, and makes money doing it. To crack the code, you have to ask the right questions.

What's the Magic Trick? (Value Proposition): What problem does this company solve so beautifully that people are willing to open their wallets? Is it convenience? Status? Pure joy? Lower costs? This is the core of its existence.

Who's in the Audience? (Target Customers): A magician doesn't perform for everyone; they perform for a specific audience. Who is this company's audience? Are they tech-savvy millennials, budget-conscious families, or Fortune 500 corporations? Knowing the who explains the what and the how.

What Happens Backstage? (Key Activities & Resources): What does the company actually do all day? Write code? Manufacture widgets? Run ad campaigns? And what are the essential props and crew members (patents, factories, brilliant engineers) it needs to pull off the show?

Who Are the Allies? (Key Partners): Batman has Robin. Frodo had Sam. Who are the company's indispensable partners? Suppliers, distributors, co-creators? These relationships can be a massive source of strength.

The Handshake and the Megaphone (Customer Relationships & Channels): How does the company connect with its audience? Is it a personal, white-glove service or a fully automated, self-serve website? And how does it get its message out and deliver the magic trick—through retail stores, a website, a direct sales force?

The Price of the Ticket & The Final Tally (Cost Structure & Revenue Streams): Finally, the bottom line. What are the biggest expenses in putting on this show? And how, exactly, does the money flow in? Is it a one-time ticket sale? A recurring subscription fee? Advertising? This reveals the economic engine of the whole operation.

Part 3: Feeling the Pulse—Revenue, Rhythms, and the Power to Name Your Price

If the business model is the soul, revenue is its heartbeat. It's the tangible proof of life. But just hearing a beat isn't enough; we need to understand its rhythm and its strength.

Reading the Rhythm of Revenue:
First, just listen. Is the heartbeat getting stronger (steady growth), is it erratic (volatile), or is it fading (decline)? How

does its rhythm compare to the other pulses in the neighborhood (competitors and the industry)? A company whose heart beats faster and stronger than its peers is a clear sign of vitality. Look closer: is this beat coming from one source or many? A company relying on one giant customer is like a heart with only one valve working—it's a risky condition.

The Engines of Growth (Revenue Drivers):
Revenue is born from a simple, elegant formula: Price×Volume. That's it. The company's ability to grow depends entirely on its ability to influence one or both of these levers.

Volume Drivers (Getting More People in the Door):

Winning the Popularity Contest: Stealing customers from rivals or grabbing a bigger slice of a growing pie (market share).

Exploring New Worlds: Expanding to new countries or new types of customers.

Launching the Next Hit Single: Releasing new products that get everyone excited again.

Making Friends and Keeping Them: How good is the company at attracting new customers and, more importantly, making them so happy they never leave?

The Vibe of the Times: Is the overall economy booming or busting? Sometimes, a rising tide lifts all boats.

The Ultimate Superpower: Pricing Power
This is perhaps the most magical, most sought-after trait a company can possess. Pricing power is the ability to raise prices without losing your customers. It's the difference

between a generic coffee stand that has to match competitors' prices and a brand like Apple or Starbucks that can command a premium because you believe what they offer is fundamentally better or different.

How do you spot this superpower? Look for these clues:

Is It a One-of-a-Kind Marvel? Does the company have something—a patent, a secret formula, a unique design—that no one else can replicate? Uniqueness grants pricing freedom.

Does the Name Itself Carry Weight? A powerful brand is a permission slip to charge more. People pay for the trust, status, and reliability the name represents.

Is the Cage Locked? (Switching Costs): How hard is it for customers to leave? If switching means losing data, retraining a whole team, or massive integration headaches, customers will tolerate price hikes just to avoid the pain of leaving.

Is It Air or Is It Caviar? (Necessity vs. Discretionary): People will complain, but they'll pay higher prices for electricity and medicine. They are far less likely to do so for a third vacation or a designer handbag. Essentials command pricing power.

By breaking down revenue into this dance between Volume and Price, and by assessing a company's superpower to control the latter, you move beyond just seeing a number. You understand the forces that give it life, and you can make a much wiser judgment about its future.

Decoding a Company's Financial Soul: A Guide for the Curious

Forget dusty ledgers and intimidating spreadsheets for a moment. Think of a company as a living, breathing thing. To truly understand its health, you need to do more than just check its pulse. You need to understand its metabolism—how it creates energy—and its agility—how it navigates the day-to-day. You also need to look at its blueprint for the future: its ambitions and how it plans to fund them.

Let's peek under the hood and explore the story told by the numbers.

The Engine Room: How a Business Creates Its Power

This is all about profitability—the raw power and efficiency of a company's core business. It's about turning a great idea into actual, spendable cash.

Gross Profit Margin: The First Spark of Creation. Imagine a baker. The gross profit margin tells you how much money is left from selling a loaf of bread after paying for the flour, water, and yeast (the "Cost of Goods Sold"). Is there a healthy chunk left over? A high margin means the baker has a great recipe, smart ingredient sourcing, or a price people are happy to pay. If this number shrinks, it's the first warning light: maybe the cost of flour is rising, or customers no longer crave that signature sourdough.

Operating Profit Margin: The True Cost of Doing Business. Now, think beyond the ingredients. The baker still has to pay rent for the shop, run the ovens, and pay the person at the counter. These are the operating expenses. The operating profit margin reveals what's left after all these daily costs are covered. It's a measure of the entire operation's health. A strong operating margin shows a well-managed bakery, not just a good baker. It's the difference between a passion project and a sustainable business.

Net Profit Margin: The "Bottom Line" Truth. This is the moment of truth. After the cost of ingredients and running the shop, the baker might also have a loan for that fancy new oven (interest) and has to set aside money for Uncle Sam (taxes). The net profit margin is the final slice of the pie that the owner actually gets to keep. It's the ultimate report card on profitability, reflecting how successfully the business navigates all its financial obligations to create wealth for its owners.

Return on Assets (ROA): The Magic of Turning "Stuff" into Profit. How good is the company at using everything it owns—from the cash in its bank account to the delivery van to the factory floor—to make money? That's ROA. A high ROA is a thing of beauty; it suggests a lean, mean, profit-making machine where every asset is pulling its weight. It's a sign of brilliant management that knows how to get the most out of what it has.

Return on Equity (ROE): The Investor's Payday. This one is personal for anyone who has invested their own money in the business. ROE asks a simple question: for every dollar the owners have put into this venture, how much profit is it generating for them? It's the ultimate measure of how effectively the company is enriching its shareholders. A high ROE is a company telling its investors, "Your faith in us is paying off. Handsomely."

Daily Agility: The Art of Managing Short-Term Finances

If profitability is the engine, working capital is the oil, coolant, and transmission fluid—the essential liquids that keep the machine running smoothly every single day. It's about managing the constant ebb and flow of cash.

The Current & Quick Ratios: The Financial Stress Test. These are your immediate safety checks. The Current Ratio (Current LiabilitiesCurrent Assets) asks: if you had to pay all your short-term bills right now, do you have enough easily accessible resources to do it? A healthy ratio (often around 1.5 to 2.0) means you can breathe easy. The Quick Ratio (Current LiabilitiesCurrent Assets−Inventory) is even stricter. It's the "acid test." It ignores inventory (which can be hard to sell in a pinch) and asks if you can cover your immediate debts with your most liquid assets. A quick ratio of 1.0 or more is like knowing you can handle a sudden storm without having to sell the furniture.

Cash Conversion Cycle (CCC): The Speed of Money. This is one of the most elegant financial metrics. It measures the time it takes for a dollar invested in inventory to travel through the entire business process and land back in your pocket as cash. It's a rhythm. A shorter CCC means the company has a fantastic tempo—it makes products, sells them, and collects the cash with lightning speed. This is a sign of a supremely efficient, cash-generating operation.

Inventory & Accounts Receivable Turnover: Keeping Things Moving. These ratios measure flow. Inventory Turnover (Average InventoryCOGS) shows how quickly products fly off the shelves. High turnover is great; it means you're not stuck with a warehouse full of last year's model. Accounts Receivable Turnover (Average Accounts ReceivableNet Credit Sales) measures how fast you collect the money you're owed. A quick collection cycle is crucial; it means customers are paying their bills on time, keeping your cash flow healthy and strong.

The Grand Blueprint: Building the Future with Smart Investments and Funding

A company's legacy is built on its long-term vision. This involves making bold bets on the future (capital investments) and wisely choosing how to pay for them (capital structure).

Plotting the Course: Big Bets and Big Projects

Net Present Value (NPV): Seeing the Future in Today's Dollars. NPV is like a financial time machine. It takes all the money a huge project (like building a new factory) is expected to make over many years and translates its value back to what it's worth today. Why? Because a dollar tomorrow is worth less than a dollar today. If the NPV is positive, the project is a green light—it's predicted to create more value than it costs. It's the gold standard for making smart, long-term decisions.

Internal Rate of Return (IRR): The Project's "Heartbeat." Forget dollars and cents for a second. The IRR tells you the project's expected annual percentage return. Think of it as the project's own internal growth rate. If this rate is higher than the company's minimum acceptable return (the "hurdle rate"), then the project is a contender. It's a quick, intuitive way to feel if an investment has a strong pulse.

Payback Period: How Fast Do We Get Our Money Back? This is the simplest, most human question of all: how long until this investment pays for itself? While it's a great measure of risk—a shorter payback is always safer—its weakness is that it ignores all the profits that might come rolling in after the payback point. It's a good first look, but not the whole story.

Fueling the Dream: The Mix of Debt and Equity

A company's capital structure is its financial architecture. How does it fund itself? By borrowing money (debt) or by using the owners' funds (equity)? The right balance is key.

Debt-to-Equity Ratio: The Leverage Meter. This ratio (Total Shareholder EquityTotal Debt) reveals how much the company is leaning on borrowed money versus its own funds. High debt is like a rocket booster—it can amplify growth when times are good. But it's also risky. If things go south, those loan payments are still due. It's a measure of financial courage, or perhaps recklessness.

Interest Coverage Ratio: The Safety Net. This ratio (Interest ExpenseEBIT) asks a critical question: how easily can the company make its interest payments? A high ratio is a sigh of relief. It means profits are many times greater than the interest owed, giving the company a huge cushion. A low ratio is a red flag; it signals that the company is skating on thin ice and could be in trouble if profits dip.

Weighted Average Cost of Capital (WACC): The True Cost of Ambition. WACC is the ultimate blended cost of a company's funding. It averages the cost of its debt (the interest rates it pays) and the cost of its equity (the return shareholders expect), weighted by how much of each it uses. A company's quest is to find the perfect mix of debt and equity that makes this WACC as low as possible. A low WACC means the company has access to cheap fuel for its growth engine, giving it a massive competitive advantage in building its future.

Industry and Competitive Analysis

1. The Art of the Map: Charting Your Business Territory

Think of your business as an expedition setting out into a vast, uncharted world. To succeed, you wouldn't just start walking and hope for the best; you'd need a map. Industry and competitive analysis is the art and science of creating that map. It's a living document that helps you understand the terrain, spot hidden treasures (opportunities), avoid treacherous pitfalls (threats), and ultimately, find your own corner of the world to build a kingdom. Sailing without this map is sailing blind, guided by nothing but guesses and gut feelings in a world that demands sharp-eyed navigation.

The first goal of this expedition is to find a good place to land. You're looking for a vibrant, thriving ecosystem, not a barren wasteland where everyone is fighting over a few scraps. This analysis helps you decide where to point your ship. Just as crucial, it forces you to look at your own crew and vessel. What are you uniquely good at? Is your ship the fastest? The strongest? Or perhaps just small and nimble enough to navigate rivers others can't? Knowing this helps you play to your strengths and patch your leaks. This process is also your weather forecast, helping you see the storm of disruption on the horizon long before it hits—think of the merchants who saw the coming age of steam and switched from sail. Ultimately, your map informs your grand strategy, whether it's to be the most powerful navy (cost leadership), the most exotic and desirable destination (differentiation), or the ruler of a small, forgotten island no one else noticed.

Crafting this strategic map is a journey in itself, with clear steps along the path.

First, you must define the borders of your map. This sounds simple, but it's vital. Are you charting the entire continent of "automobiles," or are you focused on the newly discovered volcanic island of "electric vehicles"? The scope of your map determines everything that follows.

Next, you analyze the lay of the land. The classic explorer's guide for this is Porter's Five Forces. Think of it as your survival checklist for a new territory:

Power of the Natives (Buyers): Can the locals easily demand lower prices for your goods, or are they grateful for what you bring?

Power of the Gatekeepers (Suppliers): Do you have many options for supplies, or does a single tribe control the only source of fresh water?

The Threat of New Explorers (New Entrants): How easy is it for another expedition to land on your shores and set up camp?

The Threat of Strange New Fruits (Substitutes): Could the natives suddenly decide they prefer coconuts to the bread you're offering?

Rival Expeditions (Rivalry): How many other explorers are in this area, and how fiercely are they competing for the same resources?

With the terrain understood, you identify the secrets to survival. What does it take to truly thrive here? In the jungle of smartphones, it might be relentless innovation and a near-magical supply chain. Knowing these "key success factors" tells you whether you need to be a better hunter, a better farmer, or a better diplomat to win.

Then, you begin to sketch the other players. Who are your direct rivals—the other explorers flying similar flags? And who are the indirect ones—perhaps a peaceful farming tribe that could make your trading post obsolete? You create detailed portraits of each, noting their strategies, their strengths, their Achilles' heels, and even the spirit of their crew.

You then dig deeper, deciphering their ambitions. Is that rival expedition trying to conquer the whole continent, or are they just looking for a quick profit before sailing home? Understanding their goals helps you predict their next move.

Finally, this all leads to predicting the future. If you build a new fort, how will they react? Will they build a bigger one next to it, try to cut off your supply lines, or simply sail to a different island? This foresight allows you to plan your moves and counter-moves, turning a simple map into a dynamic, strategic game board. This isn't a one-time map-making project; it's a constant process of surveying and updating, ensuring you can adapt, innovate, and flourish in a world that is always changing.

2. The Map's Legend: How We Name and Group the World

Once an explorer has sketched a territory, they need a legend—a key to make sense of the symbols. Industry classification systems are the standardized legends that allow all explorers, economists, and entrepreneurs to speak the same language. Without them, one person's "dense jungle" is another's "fertile woodland," and chaos reigns.

One of the most respected map-making guides is the North American Industry Classification System (NAICS). Think of it as the official atlas of the economic world, created by the governments of the U.S., Canada, and Mexico. It assigns a precise, six-digit coordinate to every type of economic activity. The first two digits show you the continent (e.g., 51 for the "Information" landmass), while the following digits zoom you into a specific country, region, and finally, a single town (e.g., 511110 for Newspaper Publishers). NAICS's power is its comprehensive, hierarchical structure and its commitment to staying current, adding new territories as they're discovered. It's the gold standard for government data, allowing for reliable comparisons across the map and through time.

Before NAICS, there was the Standard Industrial Classification (SIC) system. It was the old-world map, using a four-digit code. While it's less detailed and not updated anymore, you'll still find these old maps in historical archives, so knowing how to read them is a valuable skill for any seasoned explorer.

But not everyone uses the official government atlas. The financial world, a realm of high-stakes treasure hunters, often prefers the Global Industry Classification Standard (GICS). Created by MSCI and Standard & Poor's, GICS is a map designed for investors. It groups companies based on how they make their money, which is incredibly useful for comparing the performance of similar ventures. It's a more specialized map, focusing on publicly traded companies and often quicker to recognize newly formed industry islands than the slower-moving government cartographers.

Comparing these maps reveals their true purpose. NAICS is the grand, encyclopedic atlas for understanding the entire economy. GICS is the investor's treasure map, focused on profit and opportunity.

Beyond these formal legends, however, the most insightful explorers create their own custom maps. They group the world not just by official labels, but by what matters for their specific quest.

Grouping by a Shared Look: The most intuitive way is to group together companies that make the same things. All makers of telescopes belong together, as they are direct rivals in helping people see the stars.

Grouping by a Shared Customer: You might group a luxury yacht builder with a private jet manufacturer. Their products are different, but they are both trying to win the hearts (and wallets) of the world's wealthiest adventurers.

Grouping by a Shared Secret: Companies can be grouped by the secret technology or process they use. Think of all the alchemists working to turn sunlight into power, whether they use glass panels, giant windmills, or rushing water.

Grouping by a Shared Territory: Businesses that operate only in the jungles of South America face different challenges and rules than those sailing the European seas. Geography is a powerful way to frame the competitive landscape.

Grouping by a Shared Philosophy: You can group companies by how they do business. All the subscription-box merchants, for example, share a similar model, even if one sells coffee and another sells socks. Their underlying machinery is the same.

In the end, standardized maps like NAICS and GICS give you the common language to discuss the world. But it's the custom maps—drawn from the perspective of products, customers, technology, or business models—that provide the unique insights needed to out-navigate your rivals and find your own path to glory.

3. Surveying the Land: Measuring a Market's Vitals

A map is just a drawing until you add scale and data. To truly understand a territory, you must measure it—take its vital signs to assess its health, its potential, and the intensity of the struggle for control. This quantitative survey is the heartbeat of your strategic plan.

How Big is This World? (Industry Size)
First, you measure the sheer size of the territory. This is usually expressed in the total gold pieces (revenue) exchanged or the total number of goods (units) traded within its borders in a year. Is this a tiny island or a vast continent? To find out, you must become a data detective, piecing together clues from government surveys (pegged to those NAICS codes), reports from the explorers' guild (industry associations), charts from professional map-makers (market research firms), and the public ledgers of major expeditions (financial reports). Knowing the size gives you a sense of scale. A vast continent offers immense opportunity, but it may also be home to fearsome dragons.

Is This World Growing or Shrinking? (Growth Characteristics)
Next, you measure its movement. Is the coastline expanding or eroding? This is an industry's growth rate. A rapidly expanding world, like those of artificial intelligence or renewable energy, is a frontier filled with opportunity for settlers. A mature world, like the empires of packaged

goods, grows slowly, and any gains in territory must be taken from a rival. A declining world, like the land of landline telephones, is slowly sinking into the sea, its demand drying up due to changing tides of technology and taste. To chart this, you look at historical trends, but you also become a futurist, asking: What new currents of culture, technology, or regulation are shaping the future of this land?

How Fertile is the Soil? (Profitability)

This is perhaps the most fundamental question: can you prosper here? Industry profitability isn't about one explorer's lucky find; it's about the overall fertility of the soil. Does this land yield bountiful harvests with little effort, or is it a rocky desert where everyone fights for survival? High profitability means the ecosystem is rich, while low profitability suggests a brutal environment. The explorer's survival checklist (Porter's Five Forces) provides the perfect explanation: if powerful locals (buyers) can force you to trade for a pittance, or if countless rival expeditions are flooding the land, the soil will be barren for everyone. Understanding this helps you set realistic expectations for your own harvest.

Who Controls What? (Market Share Trends)

Finally, you draw the political boundaries on your map. Market share shows what percentage of the entire territory each expedition controls. More importantly, you watch how these borders shift over time. Is the old empire crumbling as a young upstart claims more and more land? Tracking these shifts reveals the true story of the power dynamics. A rising player is a threat to watch. A falling leader has a weakness you can exploit. This data, often compiled by market research firms, is the chronicle of the ongoing war for influence. A wise leader knows that sometimes it's worth sacrificing a bit of treasure (short-term profit) to capture a strategic hill (market share), knowing it will provide a dominant position for years to come.

By meticulously measuring an industry's size, growth, fertility, and the shifting lines of control, you transform your map from a simple sketch into a rich, living document. It gives you the quantitative clarity to place your bets, commit your resources, and confidently navigate the path to success.

Part 1: Your Business Isn't an Island—It's a Jungle

Before you can win the game, you have to understand the board. Every business, from the corner coffee shop to the global tech titan, operates within a wild, dynamic ecosystem. To navigate it, you need a map. Think of these two frameworks—Porter's Five Forces and PESTLE—as your satellite view and your weather forecast, giving you the lay of the land and a sense of the storms ahead.

The Five Currents of Competition (Porter's Five Forces)

Imagine your industry is a big, churning body of water. Your success doesn't just depend on how well you can swim; it depends on the currents pushing and pulling you. Michael Porter identified five of these powerful currents that define how rough the water is.

1. The Threat of New Challengers: How easy is it for someone to jump into your pool? If the pool is wide open, you'll constantly have new swimmers splashing around, competing for your space. This is a low "barrier to entry." But what if your pool has a massive wall around it, a members-only gate, and a bouncer named "Patents & Capital"? That's a high barrier to entry. The airline industry has a fortress wall—you can't just buy a 747 with your

pocket money. A new dog-walking app, on the other hand? The gate is wide open.

2. The Power of Your Customers: Who's really in charge here—you or the people who buy your stuff? Think of it like this: If you're selling water in the desert, you hold all the cards. But if you're one of a hundred identical hot dog stands on a single street, the customer is king. They can pit you against each other, demanding lower prices and extra mustard, because their cost of walking to the next stand is zero. When customers are big, few, or have tons of options, their power to squeeze your profits goes way up.

3. The Power of Your Suppliers: Now, flip the script. How much do you depend on the people who sell you your raw materials? If you're a chef famous for a rare truffle pasta, and there's only one person in the country who supplies those truffles, that supplier can basically name their price. They have you over a barrel. But if you're baking a simple cake and can buy flour from a dozen different stores, you have the power. You can shop around for the best deal.

4. The Threat of a Plot Twist (Substitutes): This isn't about your direct rival. It's not Coke vs. Pepsi. It's Coke vs. a latte, a kombucha, a sparkling water, or just turning on the tap. A substitute is a different solution to the same basic need. The movie theater isn't just competing with other theaters; its biggest rival is Netflix on the couch. The existence of a good substitute puts a hard ceiling on what you can charge before people decide to solve their problem in a completely different way.

5. The Main Event (Rivalry): This is the head-to-head clash you see every day. Is your industry a friendly tennis match or a brutal cage fight? In a fast-growing industry where everyone has a unique style, competitors can often

coexist peacefully. But in a stagnant market where all the products look the same, it can turn into a bloody, price-slashing brawl for survival. Think of the ferocious battle between smartphone makers, where every new feature is a weapon in the war for your pocket.

The Weather Report for Your World (PESTLE)

If Porter's Forces are the currents in the water, PESTLE is the weather system that affects the whole region. You can't control the weather, but you'd be a fool not to check the forecast.

Political: The government is the ultimate game master. One new law, one trade agreement, one tax hike, and the entire game can change. A decision in the capital can feel like a sudden change in wind direction, either pushing you forward or stopping you dead in your tracks.

Economic: This is the financial tide. Is it high tide, with money flowing freely and consumers spending, or low tide, with a recession pulling all the resources back out to sea? Interest rates, inflation, and unemployment aren't just numbers; they determine whether your customers feel rich or poor.

Social: This is the pulse of the people, the cultural zeitgeist. What do people care about right now? Is it wellness? Sustainability? Convenience? An aging population creates a need for different products than a baby boom. Missing a social shift is like trying to sell vinyl records the year the iPod came out.

Technological: Tech isn't a gentle breeze; it's a lightning strike that can create new worlds or turn old ones to ash. It's the force that gave us the internet, AI, and gene editing. Technology doesn't just change how we do business; it changes what business is.

Legal: These are the hard-and-fast rules of the road. Labor laws, safety standards, consumer protection—this is the official rulebook you have to play by. Ignoring it leads to penalties, and a smart player knows the rules so well they can use them to their advantage.

Environmental: This is the literal ground beneath our feet. Climate change, resource scarcity, and the call for sustainability are no longer fringe issues. They are reshaping entire industries, from cars to food to fashion. Today, being a good steward of the planet isn't just good ethics; it's becoming a requirement for survival.

Part 2: Know Thyself—Forging Your Company's Winning Identity

Once you've mapped the jungle, it's time to look in the mirror. How is your company built to survive and thrive out there? It's not enough to just exist; you need a plan, a "fighting style" that makes you stand out. This is about defining who you are and then ruthlessly assessing your own strengths and weaknesses.

Choosing Your Fighting Style: How Will You Win?

In the grand arena of business, you can't be everything to everyone. You have to choose how you'll compete. Michael Porter boils it down to three classic archetypes.

1. The Cost Leader: The Lean, Mean, Efficiency Machine. This company's mantra is "waste is the enemy." They aren't necessarily the cheapest, but they are the lowest-cost operator. They achieve this through masterful efficiency, massive scale, and a relentless war on unnecessary

expenses. Think of a budget airline or a big-box discount store. Their genius isn't in a fancy product; it's in the brilliant, streamlined machine that gets a perfectly good product to you for less. The danger? A race to the bottom, where price wars leave everyone bruised and bleeding profit.

2. The Differentiator: The Rockstar.
This company doesn't want to be the cheapest; it wants to be the only. They create something so unique, so desirable, or so beautifully designed that people will happily pay a premium. This isn't just about features; it's about brand, story, and customer experience. Think of a luxury car, a cult-favorite tech gadget, or a fashion house. Their product is a statement. The challenge is to stay cool, to keep innovating, and to convince customers that the magic is worth the price.

3. The Focus Specialist: The Niche Ninja.
This company ignores the sprawling battlefield and chooses to fight in a single, specific corner of the map. They pick a small, underserved tribe and dedicate themselves to being that tribe's absolute hero. Within that niche, they can be the low-cost option or the premium, differentiated one. Think of a company that only makes ultra-high-end vegan hiking boots or a software firm that serves only dentists. They win by knowing their tiny audience better than anyone else. The risk? Their small pond might dry up, or a giant competitor might decide they want it.

Your Company's Stat Sheet: A Brutally Honest Self-Assessment

Knowing your strategy is one thing. Knowing if it's working is another. You have to grade your own report card. Think of it like a character sheet in a role-playing game—what are your stats?

Market Share (Your Kingdom): How much of the map do you control? Are your borders expanding or shrinking? It's a quick-and-dirty measure of your influence.

Brand Strength (Your Aura): When people hear your name, what do they feel? Trust? Excitement? Apathy? A powerful brand is like an invisible shield that deflects competition and attracts followers.

Financial Performance (Your Health Bar): Are you flush with cash and ready for battle, or are you limping along, one bad quarter away from disaster? Profitability, cash flow, and growth are the vital signs of your company's health.

Customer Loyalty (Your Tribe): Do you have customers, or do you have true fans? A customer buys your product. A fan will defend you in an online argument, evangelize to their friends, and forgive you when you mess up. A loyal tribe is priceless.

Innovation (Your Arsenal): What new gadgets and secret weapons are you building in your lab? Are you inventing the future, or are you still using the same old sword while everyone else has laser guns? In many jungles, the ability to innovate is the ultimate survival skill.

Operational Efficiency (Your Inner Clockwork): How smoothly does everything run behind the scenes? Is your operation a finely tuned Swiss watch, or is it a clunky machine held together with duct tape and hope? This inner grace is what allows you to deliver on your promises.

Strategic Alliances (Your Fellowship): Who fights alongside you? Smart partnerships can give you access to new magic, new maps, or new armies. No company is an island, and the right allies can make you exponentially stronger.

Leadership & Culture (Your Soul): Finally, what is the spirit of your company? What is its personality? Is it a disciplined legion of soldiers? A quirky band of artists? A daring crew of pirates? A visionary leader and a powerful culture are the invisible forces that animate everything else, turning a good strategy into a legendary one.

Company Analysis: Forecasting

1. The Art of Seeing the Future: A Guide to Financial Forecasting

Imagine you're the captain of a ship, and your company's future is the open ocean. A financial forecast is your navigation chart. It's not a crystal ball that shows you a perfect, unchangeable destination. Instead, it's a living map, drawn with the ink of history but updated in real-time by the winds of change. It's the tool you use to steer through storms and find favorable currents.

The first rule of charting these waters is to respect the wake you've left behind. Your company's past financial statements—its income statements, balance sheets, and cash flows—are the logbooks of previous voyages. They reveal patterns, rhythms, and relationships. But you can't navigate by only looking backward. The sea is never the same twice. New technologies emerge like undiscovered islands, markets shift like powerful tides, and global events can brew up a hurricane out of a calm sky.

Your chart must also be a coherent world. Every detail must connect. This is the principle of consistency. You can't chart a course that shows you gaining speed (increasing sales) without also accounting for burning more fuel (rising costs) and needing more supplies (higher inventory). Every line on your map is tethered to the others; pull one, and the others must move in response.

Of course, no map of the future is ever perfectly accurate. The goal is to be directionally correct and to understand what happens if you get blown off course. This is where you become a storyteller of possible futures through scenario planning. You chart three voyages: the "Base

Case" is your most likely path. The "Optimistic" route is the one with perfect weather and following seas. And the "Pessimistic" journey is your plan for surviving the storm. By exploring this range of possibilities, you prepare your crew for anything.

Finally, remember that a navigation chart is useless if it's out of date. Timeliness is everything. A forecast isn't something you create once and frame on the wall. It's your GPS, constantly recalculating. When a rival ship appears on the horizon or the economic barometer drops, you must update your position and adjust your course. This constant refinement keeps your forecast from becoming a historical artifact and ensures it remains a vital tool for the journey ahead.

When it comes to the actual technique of drawing your map, you have choices. You can use a "telescope" approach (top-down), starting with the grand celestial movements—the economy, the industry, the consumer cosmos—and calculating how those gravitational pulls will affect your small ship.

Or, you can use a "microscope" approach (bottom-up), starting with the individual cells of your operation. You ask your sales crew to report on the activity at every port of call, you ask your engineers how fast the engine can run, and you piece together this granular data to build a picture of the whole vessel's potential.

The wisest captains use a hybrid of both. They look through the telescope to see the weather patterns forming out at sea, then use the microscope to check the health and readiness of their own ship and crew. And woven into all of this is the invaluable principle of human judgment—the captain's gut feeling, the seasoned wisdom that can smell rain on the wind long before it appears on any instrument.

This blend of hard data and deep experience is what separates a mere navigator from a true explorer.

2. The Heartbeat of the Business: Forecasting Your Revenues

Forecasting revenue is like trying to predict a heart's rhythm. It is the single most vital pulse in your company's body. If you misread it, every other diagnosis you make about the company's health will be flawed. The revenue forecast is the life force that drives everything else.

The simplest way to check this pulse is to listen to its history. With historical trend analysis, you're essentially saying, "If the heart has been beating at a steady 60 beats per minute, it will probably continue to do so." You look at past sales and project that rhythm forward. For a calm, mature business, this can work beautifully. But it's like assuming a resting heart rate will hold steady during a sprint—it completely misses the impact of new products, market shocks, or sudden competition.

A more insightful approach is market share analysis. Here, you stop just listening to your own heartbeat and start monitoring the health of the entire ecosystem. First, you estimate the size of the whole jungle—the total market. Then, you realistically assess what portion of that jungle your company can claim as its territory. Are you the lion, or a clever fox? This method forces you to think competitively and understand your place in the wider food chain.

You can also go straight to the source with a sales force composite. This is dispatching scouts to the front lines. Your salespeople are in the trenches, with their ears to the ground. They hear the whispers of customers, see the movements of competitors, and know the lay of the land. Aggregating their individual predictions can give you a potent, ground-level forecast. The only catch? Some scouts are eternal optimists who see a feast behind every bush, while others are cautious souls who fear a predator in every shadow.

Why not just ask the customers? Customer surveys do exactly that. It's like sending out party invitations with an RSVP. You get a sense of who intends to show up. This is incredibly valuable, especially for a new venture, but you have to remember that people's plans change. Some will be last-minute no-shows, while others might bring a friend.

For businesses built on a few large relationships, a contract-based pipeline approach is king. This isn't about guessing; it's about counting your signed deals and then playing the odds on your potential ones. You treat your sales pipeline like a poker hand, assigning probabilities to each prospective deal based on how strong it looks. It provides a clear, accountable view of the money that's already on the table and the money that might be.

And what if you're launching something brand new, sailing into completely uncharted territory? You turn to analogy forecasting. You look at the logbooks of similar voyages, whether undertaken by you or a competitor. How did the last revolutionary product in your industry perform? Your new launch may not follow the exact same path, but the old map gives you a starting point, a ghost of a coastline to aim for.

Finally, there's the 'mad scientist' method: econometric modeling. This is where you build a complex machine that tries to find the secret connections between your sales and invisible forces like consumer confidence or interest rates. When it works, it's like having a superpower. But it requires a ton of data and expertise, and if you get the formula wrong, the machine can give you beautiful, confident, and completely nonsensical answers. No matter the method, forecasting revenue is a delicate dance between data, intuition, and a deep understanding of the world you operate in.

3. Fuel, Oil, and Coolant: Forecasting Expenses and Working Capital

Once you've got a handle on the engine's power (your revenue), you have to figure out how much fuel it will burn and ensure it has the lifeblood to keep from seizing up. This is the world of operating expenses and working capital—the essential, and often overlooked, components of a healthy business machine.

First, let's talk about the fuel: operating expenses. These are the costs of keeping the lights on and the doors open. The simplest way to forecast many of these is the percentage of sales method. Think of it like a car's fuel efficiency: some costs, like sales commissions or marketing, burn faster the more you accelerate your sales. If you've historically spent 10 cents on marketing for every dollar of sales, you can use that "MPG" to project future costs.

But not every cost is tied to your speed. Your rent, insurance, and the salaries of your core office team are fixed costs. They're like your monthly car payment—it's the same whether the car sits in the garage or drives across the country. For these, you can't just use a percentage. You have to look at the actual contracts, anticipate rent hikes, or plan for new hires. A powerful way to do this is with a headcount-based approach for salaries. Instead of forecasting a vague "personnel expense," you plan your actual crew. How many people will you need? What will you pay them? This transforms a generic number into a strategic plan for your team.

Now for the oil and coolant that keep the engine running smoothly: working capital. This is the fluid financial ecosystem of your daily operations—the money customers owe you, the products waiting on your shelves, and the bills you owe to suppliers. Get this wrong, and a profitable company can still run out of cash and grind to a halt.

Accounts Receivable is the money your customers owe you. The key metric here is Days Sales Outstanding (DSO). Think of it as your "generosity window." If your DSO is 30 days, it means you're effectively giving your customers an interest-free, 30-day loan. Your forecast must account for the fact that a chunk of your sales will always be floating in this 30-day window, made but not yet spendable.

Inventory, on the other hand, is cash you've turned into physical stuff. The question, measured by Days Inventory Outstanding (DIO), is how long does that stuff sit on your shelf before it becomes cash again? If your DIO is 60 days, it means you need to have two months' worth of product costs tied up in your warehouse at all times. It's idle money, and the goal is to keep that idle time as short as possible without running out of stock.

Finally, there's Accounts Payable, which is the flip side of the coin. It's how long you take to pay your own bills. Measured by Days Payable Outstanding (DPO), this is effectively an interest-free loan from your suppliers. If you can stretch your payments to 45 days, you give yourself an extra month and a half of flexibility with your cash. It's a delicate dance—be a good partner, but manage your resources wisely.

These three elements are not independent; they are a swirling, interconnected system. More sales means more receivables. To meet those sales, you need more inventory. To get that inventory, you have more payables.

Mastering this flow is the key to ensuring your company not only has a powerful engine but also the liquidity and health to run the marathon.

The Art of the Financial Compass: Charting a Company's Future

Peering into a company's financial future is less like reading a spreadsheet and more like gazing at the stars to navigate a vast, open sea. Forecasting where you'll invest your treasure (capital investments) and how you'll fuel the journey (capital structure) is the grand art of corporate navigation. It's a blend of hard science and seasoned intuition, where the goal isn't to predict a single, certain destination, but to chart a course resilient enough for any weather.

Building the Ship: Forecasting Your Capital Investments

Capital investments, or CapEx, are the very bones and sinew of your company—the new factory, the smarter technology, the upgraded fleet. These aren't just expenses; they are the seeds of tomorrow's growth, the armor against competition, and the engine of efficiency. To forecast them is to dream up the ship you'll need for the voyage ahead.

Listening to the Crew (The Bottom-Up Approach): This journey begins in the engine room and on the deck. Your engineers, your inventors, your sales force—they have their ears to the ground. The manufacturing team knows which machine is groaning its last breath. The IT department sees the technological wave about to crest. Each department sends up its flare, a list of needs and dreams. Management then gathers these dispatches, assembling a complete picture of the ship's condition and potential, piece by meticulous piece. It's granular, deeply connected to the daily hum of the business.

The Captain's Chart (The Top-Down Approach): Sometimes, the vision comes from the crow's nest. Senior leadership declares a new destination: "We're expanding to the Western continent!" This grand strategy dictates the forecast. Suddenly, the need for new ports, larger vessels, and foreign outposts becomes the central assumption. The big picture is painted first, and the details of the necessary investments are filled in later. This ensures every dollar spent serves the ultimate quest, though it might initially overlook a leaky pipe in the galley.

Reading the Ship's Log (Historical Trend Analysis): A wise captain studies past voyages. We look at the logbooks: historically, for every league we've sailed (revenue growth), how much have we spent on new sails and rigging (CapEx)? This ratio, say 5% of revenue, becomes our starting compass point. But beware the siren song of the past. The waters ahead are never identical to the ones behind. A sudden storm or a new trade route can make old logs dangerously obsolete.

Spying on the Fleet (Industry Benchmarks): It's wise to peer through the spyglass at other ships in the fleet. Are our rivals building faster, more efficient vessels? Is our investment in cannons (R&D) and hull strength (infrastructure) on par with theirs? This provides invaluable context, ensuring we aren't caught in a nimble frigate when the rest of the fleet is building ironclads. But remember, every ship has its own unique cargo and destination; a direct comparison is a guide, not a gospel.

Mending the Sails (The Replacement Cost Method): A ship is in constant battle with the elements. Wood rots, sails tear, steel rusts. This method isn't about glamour; it's about survival. It involves methodically tracking the lifespan of every asset—from delivery trucks to data servers—and forecasting the cost to replace them before they fail. This is the unglamorous but essential work that prevents the voyage from ending in disaster.

The Grand Expedition (Project-Specific Forecasting): Then there are the once-in-a-generation voyages—the founding of a new colony, the construction of a legendary flagship. For these massive, one-off projects, we don't just use a compass; we create a detailed, three-dimensional map. We employ sophisticated financial modeling, calculating the winds and currents of future cash flows to determine if the prize is worth the risk, often using tools like Net Present Value (NPV) analysis to see if the treasure outweighs the cost of the expedition.

Fueling the Voyage: Forecasting Your Capital Structure

A ship needs fuel. Capital structure is the recipe for that fuel—the precise mix of borrowed power (debt) and owned power (equity) that propels the company forward. This blend determines your speed, your risk of running aground, and the ultimate value of your journey.

The Golden Ratio (Target Capital Structure): Many companies have a "golden ratio," a target mix of debt and equity they believe gives them the perfect balance of speed and stability. Like a ship's ballast, this ratio keeps them upright in choppy seas. The forecast, then, is simple: as the company grows, it will add debt and equity in lockstep to maintain this perfect equilibrium.

Riding the Tides (Growth Rate Projections): A company surging forward on a tide of high growth needs more fuel, and fast. The question is, where does it come from? Do we use the profits we've stored in our own tanks (retained earnings), or do we take on more from lenders (debt)? High-growth vessels often prefer to use their own reserves or invite more owners aboard (equity) to avoid being weighed down by heavy debt obligations.

The Plimsoll Line of Debt (Debt Capacity Analysis): Every ship has a Plimsoll line—a marking on the hull showing the maximum depth to which it can be safely loaded. A company's debt capacity is its financial Plimsoll line. How much debt can we take on before we risk sinking? This analysis involves stress-testing our ability to make interest payments and projecting our cash flows to see how much weight we can truly bear. Lenders are watching this line just as closely as we are.

Sharing the Spoils (Dividend Policy): When the voyage is profitable, what do we do with the treasure? Do we share it with our investors as a reward (dividends), or do we reinvest it in strengthening the ship for the journeys ahead (retained earnings)? This decision directly impacts the amount of internal equity we have to fuel future growth. A company that pays generous dividends will have less self-generated fuel and may need to look for external sources.

The Winds and the Weather (Market Conditions): No ship sails in a vacuum. The economic weather—interest rates, investor sentiment, the liquidity of the capital seas—is a powerful, uncontrollable force. When the winds of the market offer cheap borrowing, debt financing is a favorable current. When the sun shines on the stock market, raising sails to catch new equity might be the best course. A forecast must be a weather report, anticipating the changing financial climate.

The Laws of the Sea (Industry & Regulatory Factors): Different seas have different rules. Utilities, like sturdy icebreakers in predictable waters, can carry immense leverage. Tech startups, like experimental speedboats in uncharted territory, often rely on the lighter fuel of equity. New maritime laws (banking regulations) can also change how and where we are allowed to refuel, shaping our choices.

The Flight Simulator: Why Scenario Analysis is Your Most Powerful Tool

Forecasting with a single set of assumptions is like charting a course for one specific weather pattern and ignoring all others. It's a dangerous illusion of certainty. This is where scenario analysis, the financial world's flight simulator, becomes indispensable. It's the art of telling stories about the future—and preparing for all of them.

Instead of one forecast, we create a portfolio of possible futures.

Identify the Storms and Trade Winds: We begin by asking: What are the great uncertainties? These are the key drivers—economic growth, interest rate swings, a competitor's surprise move, a technological disruption. These are the variables that could send our voyage in wildly different directions.

Chart Multiple Worlds: We then build a few plausible, internally consistent stories about the future.

The "Smooth Sailing" Scenario: A world of strong economic tailwinds, low costs, and high demand.

The "Choppy Seas" Scenario: Our base case, a mix of expected challenges and opportunities.

The "Perfect Storm" Scenario: A harrowing tale of recession, supply chain chaos, and credit markets freezing over.

Sail Through Each Story: We run our ship—our financial model—through each of these simulated worlds. In the "Perfect Storm," do we slash our investment plans and hoard cash? In "Smooth Sailing," do we accelerate our expansion, perhaps taking on more debt to seize the day?

Read the Phantom Logbooks: After the simulations, we compare the outcomes. Where are our plans brittle? Where are they surprisingly resilient? If our debt level becomes unsustainable in the "Perfect Storm," we have found a critical vulnerability. If we discover a massive, untapped opportunity in the "Smooth Sailing" scenario, we have found a hidden treasure.

Build Your Life Rafts and Speed Sails: The final step is to act. Scenario analysis isn't an academic exercise; it's a call to action. It forces us to build contingency plans. We might secure a backup line of credit for the storm or pre-approve an expansion plan for the good weather. We don't know which future will come to pass, but we are now prepared for a wider range of them.

By moving beyond single-point forecasts and embracing the rich tapestry of possibilities offered by scenario analysis, we transform financial planning from a fragile act of prediction into a robust strategy of preparedness. We build a company that is not just designed for the future we expect, but is resilient enough to thrive in the future that actually arrives. We become not just forecasters, but masters of our financial destiny, ready to navigate any sea with wisdom, courage, and a well-charted course.

Equity Valuation: Concepts and Basic Tools

The Art of the Deal: Is Your Stock a Masterpiece or a Forgery?

Imagine you're not an investor, but a world-class art appraiser. You walk into a bustling, chaotic auction house—the stock market. All around you, pieces are being bought and sold in a frenzy of bids and speculation. Your job isn't to get swept up in the excitement. Your job is to find the one true masterpiece hiding in plain sight, the one whose price tag is a whisper of its real, breathtaking value.

This is the heart of investing. It's not about chasing trends; it's about understanding worth. It's about training your eye to distinguish between a fleeting fad and a timeless classic. So, how do we do it?

The Appraiser's Verdict: Priceless, Pricey, or a Perfect Price?

Before you can make a bid, you need a verdict. You study the brushstrokes, the history, the artist's potential—you determine the painting's intrinsic value. This is its soul, its fundamental truth, separate from the auction room's noise. Then, you glance at the market price, the number flickering on the electronic board. The relationship between those two numbers tells you everything.

Undervalued: The Dusty Attic Rembrandt. This is the dream. You've discovered a masterpiece whose genius is being completely overlooked. Its intrinsic value—its historical significance, its technical brilliance—is immense, yet its market price is shockingly low. This is your signal to buy with quiet confidence, knowing that sooner or later, the world will wake up and the price will soar to reflect its true glory. You found the hidden gem.

Fairly Valued: The Mona Lisa. Everyone knows this piece is a masterpiece. It's famous, its value is well-established, and its price tag is astronomical, but appropriately so. There's no bargain here, but you're paying a fair price for undeniable quality and stability. It's a solid, respectable cornerstone for any collection.

Overvalued: The Hyped-Up Souvenir. This piece is the talk of the town, driven by buzz and speculation. The bidding has become a frenzy, pushing the price to a place that has nothing to do with the quality of the art itself. Your appraiser's eye sees a simple print being sold for the price of an original. It's a bubble of perception, and bubbles are destined to pop. This is a clear signal to stay away, or if you own it, to sell to the highest bidder before the illusion shatters.

Remember, appraisal is an art, not a science. Two expert appraisers can look at the same painting and arrive at different values. The goal isn't to find a single, perfect number, but to build a strong, evidence-based case for the value you see.

The Appraiser's Toolkit: Uncovering True Worth

So how do we calculate that elusive intrinsic value? We don't just guess; we use a toolkit of powerful models, each offering a different lens through which to view the company.

1. The Crystal Ball Method (Discounted Cash Flow Models)

This is the most fundamental approach. It operates on a simple, magical premise: a business is worth the sum of all the cash it will ever generate in the future. The trick is that a dollar tomorrow is worth less than a dollar today. So, we use a "discount rate" (think of it as a reverse interest rate) to pull all of that imagined future cash back to the present day to see what it's worth right now.

Dividend Discount Model (DDM): Focuses only on one kind of cash: the dividends paid out to shareholders. It's like valuing a fruit tree based only on the fruit you expect to harvest each year.

Free Cash Flow (FCF) Models: This is a more holistic view. It values the entire cash-generating engine of the company—all the money flowing through it before it gets sliced up for shareholders or debt payments. It's like valuing the entire orchard, not just the fruit.

This method is powerful, but it's a crystal ball. Your valuation is only as good as your predictions about the future. A slightly more optimistic or pessimistic guess about growth can dramatically change the result.

2. The Neighborhood Watch Method (Relative Valuation)

This is the most popular, "street-smart" approach. Instead of gazing into the future, you just look around the neighborhood. You value a company by comparing it to its peers. How is this company priced compared to its direct competitors?

Price-to-Earnings (P/E) Ratio: Share Price / Earnings Per Share. The classic. It asks, "How much is the market willing to pay for every dollar this company earns?" A high P/E is a vote of confidence in future growth.

Price-to-Book (P/B) Ratio: Share Price / Book Value Per Share. Compares the price to the company's net worth on paper. It's like comparing a house's market price to what it cost to build it.

Price-to-Sales (P/S) Ratio: Share Price / Revenue Per Share. Perfect for exciting young companies that aren't yet profitable. It ignores earnings and asks, "How much are people paying for every dollar of this company's sales?"

EV/EBITDA: The professional's choice. It strips away the noise of debt and accounting quirks to compare the raw operating horsepower of different businesses. It's the most "apples-to-apples" comparison you can get.

The catch? If the entire neighborhood (the whole industry) is in a real estate bubble, this method will just confirm the inflated prices. It tells you if you're overpaying relative to others, not if everyone is overpaying together.

3. The Scrap Yard Method (Asset-Based Valuation)

This is the most brutally honest approach. It asks, "If this company shut its doors today and sold everything—its factories, its desks, its inventory—what would all the pieces be worth?" This gives you a liquidation value, a hard floor below which the company's stock price should never fall. It's a valuation of last resort, best for industrial giants and less useful for tech companies whose greatest assets (code, brand) are intangible.

The Company's Language: How They Return Value

Once you own a piece of a company, how does it say "thank you" for your investment? Companies have several ways to return profits to their shareholders or adjust their stock's architecture.

1. The Cash in Hand (Dividends)

Regular Cash Dividends: This is the classic. A reliable, predictable cash payment deposited into your account, usually every quarter. It's the company sharing its profits directly with you, its part-owner.

Extra Dividends: A surprise party! The company had a spectacular year or sold a big asset, and it's sharing the windfall. It’s a one-time bonus, a "special dividend" that shouldn't be expected to repeat.

2. The Share Shuffle (Stock Splits & Dividends)

Stock Dividends: Instead of cash, the company gives you more shares. If you own 100 shares, a 5% stock dividend gives you 5 new shares. The catch? The company’s total value hasn’t changed, so the price per share drops proportionally. It's like getting more, smaller slices of the same pizza.

Stock Splits: The company declares that every share you own is now two (a 2-for-1 split). The goal is purely psychological: to cut a high share price in half to make it seem more affordable to smaller investors. Your $100 stock becomes two $50 stocks. Your total investment value is unchanged.

Reverse Stock Splits: The opposite. The company is worried its stock price is too low (say, $0.50), making it look cheap and risky. So it declares a 1-for-10 reverse split. Your 1,000 shares at $0.50 each become 100 shares at $5.00 each. It's an attempt to regain a look of respectability, though the underlying value hasn't changed.

3. The Stealth Maneuver (Share Repurchases)

This is perhaps the most popular modern method. Instead of sending cash to shareholders, the company uses its cash to buy its own stock from the open market. This is a masterstroke for a few reasons:

It reduces the number of shares out there, making your remaining shares rarer and more valuable.

With fewer shares, the company's Earnings Per Share (EPS) automatically goes up, making the business look more profitable on paper.

It functions like a dividend but allows investors to defer taxes until they sell their shares.

Think of it as the company betting on itself. By reducing the supply of its own stock, it sends a powerful signal that management believes the shares are undervalued—a secret handshake to the savvy investor.

The Art of Value: A Company's Financial Performance

Imagine a company not as a cold, corporate machine, but as a living performer on the world's economic stage. It has its own rhythm, its own story, and its own way of rewarding its audience—the shareholders. Understanding this performance is the art of investing. It's about more than just numbers; it's about deciphering the choreography of its cash, appreciating its potential, and ultimately deciding if the show is worth the price of admission.

Act I: The Dividend Ballet - A Rhythmic Reward

When a successful company decides to share its profits, it doesn't just toss cash into the crowd. It performs a carefully choreographed ballet, a four-step sequence where every date holds a special meaning for the audience.

The performance begins with the Declaration Date. Picture the house lights dimming and the company's board of directors stepping onto the stage. They announce their intention, making a public promise: "We will pay a dividend." They state the amount, perhaps fifty cents for every seat you hold, and set the dates for the rest of the show. A press release sounds the opening chord, and the market leans in, anticipating the next move.

Next comes the most crucial step for any aspiring audience member: the Ex-Dividend Date. Think of this as the "velvet rope" moment. To receive the promised payout, you must own your ticket (the stock) before this date. The stock exchange, acting as the ultimate event organizer, sets this date to ensure everyone knows who's on the guest list. If you buy on or after the ex-dividend date, the dividend belongs to the seller; you've arrived just after the cutoff for this particular party. This is why on the ex-dividend date, the stock's price often takes a small dip, roughly equal to the dividend itself—the ticket price no longer includes that specific payout.

Following this is the Record Date. This is the moment the house lights come up and the company takes a snapshot of its audience. The company's transfer agent freezes the guest list, officially noting every shareholder registered as an owner. If you bought your ticket before the ex-dividend date, your name is on that list, circled in gold. You are officially "of record."

Finally, the grand finale: the Payment Date. The promise is fulfilled. The company sends out the cash, whether as a check in the mail or a direct deposit that magically appears in your account. This is the tangible applause, the concrete reward for your faith in the performance. It's the moment the value is transferred from the stage directly into your hands.

Act II: The Critic's Toolkit - How to Value the Performance

So, how do you, the discerning investor, determine what a company's stock is truly worth before the show? You need a critic's toolkit, and the most foundational tools are built on a single, profound idea: the time value of money. A dollar in your pocket today is a powerful tool; a dollar promised next year is just a whisper on the wind, weakened by inflation and missed opportunities. To value any asset, you must pull all its expected future cash flows back through time to see what they're worth today. It's like having a financial time machine.

The Dividend Discount Model (DDM): The Classical Approach

The DDM is the most traditional and intuitive form of criticism. It posits that a stock's true value is simply the sum of all the future dividends it will ever pay, discounted back to the present. It's a valuation of pure trust and tangible returns.

The blueprint for this looks like:
$P0=t=1 \Sigma \infty (1+r)tDt$

Where P0 is today's value, Dt is the dividend in a future period, and r is the discount rate reflecting the risk.

Since forecasting to infinity is a bit much, the elegant Gordon Growth Model (GGM) simplifies this for mature, steady performers who grow their dividend at a constant pace.

Its formula is a masterpiece of simplicity:

$P0=r-gD1$

Here, D1 is next year's dividend, and g is the constant, gentle growth rate. This model sees value in consistency and predictable rewards, much like a critic who appreciates a flawless classical ballet.

The Free Cash Flow to Equity (FCFE) Model: The Modernist View

But what about the brilliant, rebellious performers who don't pay dividends? What about the innovative tech company that pours every penny back into its craft, promising a future masterpiece? The FCFE model is the critic's lens for them. It ignores the declared dividend and instead measures the total cash the company could, in theory, hand over to shareholders after funding its operations and growth. It's a measure of raw, untapped potential.

FCFE is the cash left over after all the bills are paid and all necessary investments in the future are made. The valuation principle is the same: forecast this "free cash" into the future and discount it back to today.
$P0=t=1\sum\infty(1+r)tFCFEt$

This model doesn't care about the company's current dividend policy. It peers behind the curtain, into the engine room, to measure the true power being generated. It values the potential to create wealth, not just the willingness to distribute it.

Act III: Choosing Your Lens - The Strengths and Limits of Criticism

No single critical lens is perfect for every performance. A savvy investor knows when to use a magnifying glass and when to use a telescope.

The Dividend Discount Model is a beautifully crafted but rigid ruler.

Its Genius: For the rock-solid, blue-chip company with a history of rewarding shareholders like clockwork, the DDM is pure, simple, and connected to the reality of what you actually receive in your pocket. It speaks the language of tangible returns.

Its Blind Spot: It is utterly useless for valuing the vast universe of companies that don't pay dividends. For the young, disruptive growth company, the DDM sees a blank stage and assigns it no value. Furthermore, its reliance on a constant growth rate can feel like trying to fit a dynamic, living entity into a perfectly straight line—a tiny shift in that assumed line can drastically alter the entire valuation.

The Free Cash Flow to Equity Model is a powerful but demanding X-ray machine.

Its Genius: It can see the potential in any company, dividend-paying or not. It cuts through accounting conventions to look at the hard, cold cash a business generates, making it a more holistic and flexible tool. It values the innovators and the empire-builders based on their fundamental strength.

Its Blind Spot: This power comes at a cost. Forecasting all the moving parts of FCFE—capital projects, working capital needs, debt strategies—is like trying to predict a jazz musician's every future solo. It's complex, messy, and a single wrong note in your forecast can throw off the entire composition. The results can be volatile and are heavily dependent on the analyst's skill and assumptions.

In the end, valuing a company is less a science and more a craft. It requires choosing the right tools, understanding their limitations, and blending analytical rigor with a feel for the story the company is telling. The best investors are like the most insightful critics; they appreciate the nuances of the performance, see the potential behind the curtain, and know, with confidence, when to give a standing ovation.

1. The Financial Golden Goose: Finding the True Worth of a Forever Stock

Let's talk about finding a stock's soul. Not its flashy market price that flitters up and down with the day's news, but its deep, intrinsic value. Imagine you're not buying a piece of paper, but a promise. When it comes to a non-callable, non-convertible preferred stock, that promise is one of the purest you can find.

Think of it like buying a magical goose. This isn't just any goose; it's a special breed that lays a golden egg of a specific size, at the same time, every single year, forever.

The Golden Egg: This is your Annual Preferred Dividend. It's a fixed, predictable cash payment. If the goose's "par value" is $100 and it has a 5% "egg-laying rate," you know you're getting a $5 golden egg every year. No surprises, no drama. It's the steady heartbeat of your investment.

Your "Is It Worth It?" Number: This is the Required Rate of Return. This part is all about you. It's the personal yardstick you use to measure any investment. What influences it? Well, what if your neighbor is selling a goose that lays silver eggs that are growing in value? (That's the competition from other investments like bonds). What if this golden goose looks a little frail? (That's the company's credit risk). You have to decide the minimum annual return that makes buying this specific goose worthwhile for you.

So, how much should you pay for this magical, forever-goose? The formula is beautifully simple:

Price of the Goose = Size of the Golden Egg / Your "Is It Worth It?" Number

Let's say our goose lays a $4 golden egg each year. You've looked at other opportunities and decided you need at least a 6% return on your money to feel good about this deal.

Value = $4 / 0.06 = $66.67

That's it. Your personal, fair price for this goose is $66.67. If the farmer is selling it for $60, you've found a bargain. If they're asking $75, you might walk away, because it doesn't meet your standards.

The "non-callable" part is crucial—it means the farmer can't suddenly decide to buy the goose back from you. And "non-convertible" means it won't magically transform into a chicken (common stock) overnight. This certainty is what makes the valuation so clean and powerful. You are buying a simple, elegant, perpetual stream of golden eggs.

2. The Dividend Tree: Valuing a Company's Growth Story

When we turn to common stocks, the game changes. We're no longer buying a goose that lays the same egg forever. We're planting a tree. And that tree is expected to grow, producing more fruit (dividends) over time. How we value that tree depends on what kind of tree it is.

The Old-Growth Oak: The Gordon (Constant) Growth Model

Imagine a magnificent, mature oak tree in the middle of a forest. It's been there for decades. It's not going to double in size overnight, but you can count on it to grow a little taller and a little wider, steadily and reliably, year after year. This is the kind of company the Gordon Growth Model is built for.

It's a company that has settled into a comfortable rhythm, growing its dividend at a slow, sustainable pace forever. To find its value, you're essentially calculating the worth of all the fruit it will ever produce, from now until the end of time.

Value of the Oak = Next Year's Fruit / (Your Required Return - The Tree's Growth Rate)

Next Year's Fruit (D1): The dividend you expect to see in one year.

Your Required Return (r): Your personal "Is It Worth It?" number for owning this piece of the forest.

The Tree's Growth Rate (g): The slow, steady pace at which the tree (and its fruit production) expands each year.

This model is a vote for stability. It sees value not in explosive potential, but in relentless, predictable consistency. It's perfect for the giants of industry—the blue-chip companies that are intertwined with the economy itself.

The Ambitious Sapling: The Two-Stage Dividend Model

Now, picture a different kind of tree: a young, vibrant sapling planted in fertile soil. For the next few years, it's going to be a rocket ship. It will shoot upwards, sprouting new branches at a dizzying pace. You can't use the old oak tree formula for this; it would break the math. This sapling's growth is just too fast.

This is where the Two-Stage Model shines. It lets us tell a story in two parts.

Act I: The Growth Spurt. For the first few years, we treat the sapling like the unique specimen it is. We forecast its explosive growth year by year, calculating the value of the fruit it produces during this initial, supercharged phase.

Act II: Settling Down. We know this frantic growth can't last forever. Eventually, our sapling will mature. It will find its place in the forest and settle into the steady, predictable growth of an old oak. So, at the end of its growth spurt, we use the Gordon Growth Model to calculate its value for the rest of its life—its "happily ever after" value.

The total intrinsic value is the sum of these two parts: the value of the wild, youthful sprint, plus the value of the calm, mature marathon that follows. This model gives us the flexibility to value dynamic companies with a compelling story—a story of transformation from a high-growth prodigy into a stable, mature giant.

3. Choosing Your Story: Which Company Fits Which Model?

The art of valuation isn't just about crunching numbers; it's about seeing a company for what it is and choosing the story that fits.

The Town Elder: A Fit for the Constant Growth Model

Think of a company that is like the wise, respected elder of the business world.

Their Story: They are titans of their industry—the Coca-Colas, the Johnson & Johnsons, the major utilities. They've been around the block. Their days of explosive, world-conquering growth are behind them.

Their Character: Their defining trait is stability. They have a long, unbroken history of sharing their profits (paying dividends). Their growth is modest, often tracking the economy itself. They are predictable, reliable, and their promises are their bond. You don't invest in them for a thrilling plot twist; you invest in them for the comfort of a steady, unfolding narrative. The Gordon Growth Model, with its assumption of perpetual, steady growth, is their perfect biography.

The Ambitious Prodigy: A Fit for the Multistage Model

Now, think of a company that is the brilliant, energetic upstart, ready to change the world.

Their Story: This could be a tech firm with a revolutionary product, a biotech company whose new drug is about to hit the market, or any business that is in a phase of rapid expansion. Their story is one of dramatic, but finite, growth.

Their Character: Their defining trait is evolution. Right now, they are reinvesting heavily to fuel their meteoric rise. Their dividend growth might be huge for the next five or ten years. But we, as savvy observers, know this pace is a temporary chapter. We can foresee a time when their market matures, when competitors catch up, and when they will transition from a sprinter to a marathoner. The multistage model is the only way to properly tell this two-part story, capturing both their fiery youth and their eventual, calmer maturity. It acknowledges that their future has more than one act.

Ultimately, valuing a stock is about understanding its personality. Is it the steady Town Elder, whose value lies in its unwavering consistency? Or is it the Ambitious Prodigy, whose value is a thrilling combination of a near-term explosion and a long-term stabilization? By matching the company's character to the right valuation story, you move beyond simple math and into the true art of investing.

1. The Art of Seeing Value: A Guide to Price Multiples

Figuring out what a company is truly worth can feel like trying to catch a ghost. You can chase it with spreadsheets and complex models until you're dizzy, or you can try a more intuitive approach: you can see how it's valued by its neighbors.

The Neighborhood Watch of Investing

At its core, using price multiples is a lot like figuring out the price of a house. You wouldn't start by calculating the net present value of all potential future rental income, factoring in roof repairs and property taxes for the next 30 years. That's madness for a first look.

Instead, you'd walk the neighborhood. You'd see what the charming three-bedroom on the corner sold for. You'd check the price per square foot of the new modern build down the street. You're not just comparing houses; you're comparing stories, curb appeal, and the "vibe" of the block.

Price multiples do the same for stocks. They are the financial equivalent of a "price per square foot" or "price per bedroom," allowing you to quickly see if a company looks like a mansion priced as a bungalow, or a shack with an outrageous price tag. They are simple, fast, and soak up the mood of the entire market, telling you what investors are excited about, what they're scared of, and where they see the future heading.

The P/E Ratio: Reading a Company's Story

The Price-to-Earnings (P/E) ratio is the most famous multiple of all—the headline star. It's simply the stock price divided by the company's annual earnings per share. But what does it really tell us?

Think of a P/E ratio as the market's review of a company's story. A high P/E is like a best-selling thriller that everyone is clamoring to read. Readers (investors) are so excited about the plot twists to come (future growth) that they're willing to pay a premium for the book today. They believe the story is high-quality and the author (the company) is a genius.

A low P/E is like a dusty classic on a forgotten shelf. Is it a hidden masterpiece waiting to be rediscovered (undervalued)? Or is the story just... boring, with no growth and a predictable, unhappy ending (a company in trouble)?

The story's quality depends on three key plot devices:

The Payout: How much of the profit (the "story's royalties") does the company share with its readers (you)? A generous author is often more popular.

The Growth: This is the most thrilling part of the plot. How fast is the story's universe expanding? The more explosive the expected growth, the more people are willing to pay upfront to be a part of it.

The Risk: What are the chances the story falls flat? A risky, unpredictable plot might demand a lower price to entice readers. This "required rate of return" is your personal need to be compensated for the risk that the story doesn't have a happy ending.

So, a P/E isn't just a number; it's the market's collective imagination, pricing in a company's past performance and its future promise.

2. The Investor's Toolkit: Decoding the Key Multiples

To get a true picture of a company, you can't just use one tool. You need a full kit, with each multiple telling you something different, like a detective using various lenses to examine a clue.

The P/E Ratio: The Headline Grabber

What it is: Price / Earnings

Its Personality: This is the celebrity of multiples—famous, widely quoted, and the first thing many people look at. It tells you how much hype, hope, and expectation is baked into the stock price relative to its current profits. But like any celebrity, its public image isn't always the full story.

The P/OCF Ratio: The Truth Serum

What it is: Price / Operating Cash Flow

Its Personality: Cash doesn't lie. While earnings can be shaped by accounting rules and clever tactics, cash flow is the hard, cold reality of money moving in and out of the business. This multiple cuts through the noise and asks the ultimate question: "Forget what you say you earned, show me the money!" It's the closest you can get to a financial truth serum.

The P/S Ratio: The Dream Catcher

What it is: Price / Sales

Its Personality: This multiple is for the dreamers, the visionaries, the companies that are long on ambition but maybe short on profits. Think of a revolutionary tech startup or a biotech firm on the cusp of a breakthrough. They might not be making money yet, but boy, are they making sales. The P/S ratio values the dream, telling you how much investors are willing to pay for every dollar of that potential.

The P/B Ratio: The Pawn Shop Test

What it is: Price / Book Value

Its Personality: This is the ultimate reality check. Imagine the company goes out of business tomorrow. They have a giant yard sale, selling off every desk, factory, and truck they own. After they pay off all their debts, what's left for the shareholders? That's the book value. The P/B ratio tells you if you're buying the company for more or less than its "pawn shop" value. A P/B below 1.0 means you're theoretically buying assets for pennies on the dollar—a potential bargain hunter's delight.

3. The All-In Price: Understanding Enterprise Value

When you buy a used car, the price isn't just what you pay the owner. If the car has an outstanding loan, you're taking that on, too. The real cost is the sticker price plus the debt.

Enterprise Value (EV) is the "all-in" price for a company. It's what an acquirer would truly have to pay to own the whole business, free and clear. It's calculated as the company's market cap, plus all of its debt, minus the cash it has sitting in the bank (because you can use that cash to pay down the debt).

EV = Market Cap + All Debt - Cash

EV multiples are powerful because they ignore how a company finances itself, giving you a pure, apples-to-apples comparison. They look past the financial engineering to see the raw business underneath.

EV/EBITDA: The Engine's True Horsepower

What it is: Enterprise Value / EBITDA

Its Personality: Think of EBITDA (Earnings Before Interest, Taxes, Depreciation, and Amortization) as the raw, untamed horsepower of a company's engine. It's the pure operational power before the bean counters (taxes), bankers (interest), and asset accountants (depreciation) take their cut. The EV/EBITDA multiple tells you how much you're paying for each unit of that raw operational horsepower. It's the best way to compare the engines of a Ford and a Ferrari without getting distracted by their different financing deals or tax jurisdictions.

From "All-In" Price to Your Slice of the Pie
The magic of EV multiples is that they let you work backward to find the value of the shares.

Find the "All-In" Price: Use a comparable EV/EBITDA multiple to estimate the target company's total Enterprise Value.

Settle the Debts: From that total value, subtract the company's debts and add its cash. It's like buying that car—you pay the "all-in" price, then you use the cash in the glove box to help pay off the loan.

Find Your Slice: What's left over is the Equity Value—the value belonging to shareholders. Divide that by the number of shares, and you have your estimated price per share.

4. The Yard Sale Valuation: When Assets Are All That Matter

Sometimes, a company isn't about a grand future story or a powerful earnings engine. Sometimes, it's just about the stuff it owns. This is where asset-based valuation comes in—it's the financial equivalent of a liquidation sale.

The Core Idea: What's It All Worth?

The method is brutally simple: Imagine the company closes its doors and puts a price tag on every single thing in its possession—its land, buildings, machinery, inventory, and even its patents. You add up the market value of all that stuff, then you pay off all its debts and I.O.U.s.

The cash left in the drawer at the end of the day is the company's equity value.

When Do You Host a Yard Sale?

This approach isn't for valuing a thriving artist based on their future masterpieces. It's for valuing the canvases, paints, and easels left in their studio if they decide to quit for good. It's most useful for:

Businesses that are more "what they have" than "what they do," like real estate firms (value = buildings) or natural resource companies (value = oil in the ground).

Companies in distress or on the brink of bankruptcy, where liquidation is a real possibility.

Establishing a "floor value." For any company, the asset value represents a theoretical rock bottom. The stock price shouldn't fall below what you could get by selling everything off.

The Achilles' Heel: You Can't Price Magic

The great challenge of the "yard sale" method is putting a price tag on the intangible. How do you value a secret recipe, a beloved brand name, a brilliant corporate culture, or the trust a company has built over 50 years?

You can't. Asset-based models are terrible at capturing the synergistic magic that makes a business a living, breathing entity. They see the instruments, but they can't hear the music.
Because of this, asset-based value is often just a starting point—a conservative, tangible baseline that anchors your analysis before you look to the sky to value a company's dreams.

Subject 2: Fixed Income

Fixed-Income Instrument Features

Imagine you're not just buying a financial product, but entering into a very serious, long-term relationship. A fixed-income security, at its heart, is exactly that: a formal, binding promise between you, the lender, and a company or government, the borrower. You give them your capital, and in return, they make a solemn vow to give you a steady stream of affection (interest payments) and, at the end of it all, return your original commitment (the principal).

This relationship has its own language of love and clear-cut rules, all designed to build trust and ensure nobody gets their heart—or wallet—broken.

The First Handshake: Defining the Relationship

Before you commit, you agree on the basics. This is the simple, upfront part of the deal.

The Commitment (Face Value): This is the core amount of your loan, typically $1,000. It's the money you'll get back on the "breakup day" when the relationship term ends. It's the anchor of the entire arrangement.

The Steady Affection (Coupon Rate): This is the fixed rate of "I'm thinking of you" payments you'll receive. A $1,000 commitment with a 5% coupon rate means you get $50 a year, often split into two $25 payments. It's the reliable, predictable proof of their obligation to you.

The "Until..." Date (Maturity Date): Every relationship has a timeline. This is the predetermined date when the term is over, and your original commitment is returned to you in full. It could be a short fling of a few months or a lifelong partnership spanning decades.

The Prenup: Understanding the Bond Indenture

Now, this isn't a casual affair built on a flimsy handshake. It's governed by a powerful, legally binding document called the bond indenture. Think of it as the most detailed prenuptial agreement imaginable. It's a dense rulebook meticulously crafted to protect you, the investor. It lays out every promise, every boundary, and every "what if" scenario.

A neutral third party, called a trustee (think of them as the relationship counselor), is appointed to hold the borrower accountable and make sure they stick to the vows laid out in this document.

The Vows: Covenants, The Promises That Matter

The most human part of this indenture is the set of promises, or covenants, the borrower makes. These aren't just legal jargon; they are the fundamental rules of engagement that define the health and safety of your investment. They come in two flavors: the "I will's" and the "I will not's."

The "I Will..." Vows (Affirmative Covenants)

These are the promises of proactive care and responsibility. The borrower is vowing to be a good partner by actively maintaining their health and transparency.

"I will be an open book." The borrower promises to keep meticulous financial records and share them with you (via the trustee). No secrets.

"I will pay my dues." They vow to pay their taxes and other bills on time, preventing outside claims from jeopardizing the assets you both rely on.

"I will protect our home." They promise to keep their essential assets insured. If a fire burns down their factory, there's a safety net to protect their ability to pay you back.

"I will stay in business." They commit to maintaining their corporate existence, ensuring they continue to be a living, breathing entity capable of earning money to fulfill their promise to you.

The "I Will Not..." Vows (Negative Covenants)

These are the crucial boundaries set to prevent reckless or selfish behavior. The borrower is promising to avoid actions that could put the entire relationship at risk.

"I will not go on a borrowing spree." This is a huge one. They promise not to take on mountains of new debt that could compromise their ability to pay you, their existing partner.

"I will not drain our bank account for my friends." They agree to limit how much cash they hand out to shareholders (as dividends). This ensures cash is preserved for you first.

"I will not sell the furniture to fund a gambling habit." This covenant restricts them from selling off vital assets that are the foundation of their business, protecting the core value you invested in.

"I will not merge with a deadbeat without your say-so." They agree to limit who they merge with or acquire, preventing them from tying their fate to a riskier partner that could drag them down.

When Life Happens: The Shifting Dynamics

Even in the most structured relationship, feelings and circumstances can change.

Your Attractiveness on the Market (Market Price & Yield): While your coupon rate is fixed, the world changes. If new relationships (bonds) start offering a better deal (higher interest rates), your commitment suddenly looks less attractive. To entice someone else to take it off your hands, you'd have to sell it for less than you paid. This is the inverse dance of prices and interest rates. Your yield is the true measure of your return, blending the steady coupon payments with this fluctuating market price.

Trustworthiness (Credit Quality): How reliable is your partner, really? Rating agencies act like private investigators, assigning a score to the borrower's creditworthiness. A top-rated, "investment-grade" borrower is a rock-solid partner. A "high-yield" or "junk" borrower is a bit of a wild card—they offer you a much higher coupon rate, but there's a greater risk they might just skip town.

The Escape Hatches (Callable & Putable Bonds): Some relationships come with pre-planned exit strategies. A callable bond gives the borrower the right to end things early, usually because they found a way to "refinance" at a better rate. They pay you back your principal, but you lose out on future interest payments. A putable bond is your escape hatch—it gives you the right to demand your money back early if you see red flags, like their credit quality tanking.

In the end, investing in a fixed-income security is an act of calculated trust. By understanding its structure not as a series of cold terms, but as a relationship with clear vows and boundaries, you can better appreciate the intricate dance of risk and reward that defines this cornerstone of the financial world.

Fixed-Income Cash Flows and Types

1. The Symphony of a Bond: Understanding its Rhythms and Surprises

At its heart, a bond isn't just a financial instrument; it's a promise. It's a story about money, time, and trust, written in the language of cash flows. But not all these stories are told the same way. Some are simple, steady ballads, while others are complex symphonies with unexpected crescendos and dramatic pauses.

The Basic Rhythms:

Imagine you're planting a money tree. With a zero-coupon bond, you plant one seed (your initial investment, say $900) and walk away. You don't water it or prune it. You just wait. Years later, you return to find it has grown into a full $1,000. It's the ultimate "set it and forget it" promise, a silent partner working for you in the background. Your profit is that final, satisfying bloom. This silent patience makes it perfect for goals far on the horizon, like a child's education or your own golden years, because there's no fussing with reinvesting small bits of interest along the way.

Then there's the familiar workhorse: the coupon bond. This is less like a single tree and more like an orchard that yields fruit every season. You loan a company or government $1,000, and in return, they don't just promise your money back someday—they send you a small "thank you" check every six months. These checks, the coupons, are your reward for being a patient lender. It's a steady, predictable rhythm, a financial heartbeat that provides a reliable income stream, much like a landlord collecting rent. When the lease is up (at maturity), you get your original deposit back.

But what if you wanted to get your principal back piece by piece? Enter the amortizing bond. Think of a mortgage. Every single payment you make is a cocktail of two ingredients: a splash of interest and a healthy pour of the original loan principal. With each payment, the IOU shrinks. For the borrower, this makes the final payment less daunting. For the investor, it's a disciplined return of capital, giving them a steady flow of cash to put to work elsewhere.

Finally, we have the chameleon of the bond world: the floating-rate note (FRN). Its promise isn't set in stone. Instead, its interest payments are tied to a market benchmark, like SOFR. It dances to the rhythm of the economy. When interest rates in the market salsa upwards, your coupon payments join the dance. When they slide down, so does your income. This makes FRNs a shield against rising interest rates, but it also turns your steady income stream into an unpredictable river.

The Plot Twists: Contingency Provisions

Just when you think you know the story, a bond can hit you with a plot twist. These "what if" clauses, or contingency provisions, can rewrite the ending, sometimes in your favor, sometimes not.

Provisions for the Issuer (The Borrower's Escape Hatch)

The most famous of these is the call provision. Imagine you loaned someone money at 7% interest, but a year later, banks are only charging 4%. The borrower would feel pretty silly, right? A call provision is their "get out of jail free" card. It gives the issuer the right to forcibly buy back your bond before it's supposed to mature. They can then turn around and borrow new money at the cheaper 4% rate. For the issuer, it's a brilliant cost-saving move. For you, the investor, it's a disappointment. Your beautiful, high-paying investment is suddenly snatched away, and you're left with a pile of cash to reinvest in a world of lower returns.

A cousin to the call is the sinking fund provision. This is the issuer acting like a responsible homeowner, putting money aside to pay down the mortgage early. The provision requires the company to retire a portion of its bonds each year. While this makes the company look safer (reducing the risk of a massive default at the end), it means your specific bond could be chosen in a lottery for early retirement, creating the same reinvestment headache as a call.

Provisions for the Investor (The Empowerment Button)

But investors have their own tricks up their sleeve. The put provision is your eject button. It's the mirror image of a call. This time, you have the power. If you're holding a bond paying 3%, and new bonds are being issued at 6%, you can march back to the issuer and say, "I'd like my money back, please." The put provision forces them to buy the bond back from you at a set price. This protects you from being stuck in a low-paying investment when better opportunities arise.

Then there's the ultimate hybrid, the secret agent of the bond world: the convertible bond. It starts its life as a respectable, predictable bond, paying its coupons on time. But it carries a hidden superpower: the ability to transform into a pre-set number of the company's stock shares. If the company is doing okay, you can just enjoy the safety of the bond. But if the company's stock suddenly takes off for the moon, you can hit the conversion button, trade in your bond, and ride the rocket ship of stock appreciation. It's the "have your cake and eat it too" security—the safety of a bond with the thrilling upside of a stock.

2. The Unseen Hand: Rules, Referees, and the Taxman in the Bond Market

Investing in fixed-income is more than a two-player game between borrower and lender. It's a bustling ecosystem with a sacred rulebook (law), sharp-eyed referees (regulators), and a partner who always takes a cut (the taxman). Understanding these forces is the difference between navigating the market with a map and stumbling through it blindfolded.

The Legal Bedrock: The Bond's Constitution

Every bond is born from a legally binding contract, a "sacred scroll" known as the indenture. This document is the bond's constitution, detailing every promise, right, and obligation. Buried within are covenants, the solemn vows made by the issuer. Think of them as a "To-Do List" (affirmative covenants, like maintaining good financial health) and a "Thou Shalt Not" list (negative covenants, like not taking on a mountain of new debt). These vows protect bondholders by keeping the issuer on the straight and narrow. If the issuer breaks a vow, it's a default—and bondholders can legally demand their money back, now.

The law also dictates the pecking order in a disaster. If the company goes bankrupt, who gets a spot on the lifeboats first? Holders of secured bonds are like first-class passengers; their claim is backed by specific collateral, like buildings or equipment, giving them priority. Holders of unsecured bonds (debentures) are in steerage. They are only paid from what's left after the secured creditors take their share. This legal hierarchy is a fundamental measure of a bond's risk.

The Regulatory Referees: Ensuring a Level Playing Field

To prevent the market from becoming a rigged casino, regulatory bodies like the Securities and Exchange Commission (SEC) act as referees. Their prime directive is transparency. Before a company can ask the public for millions in loans, the SEC requires it to "show its homework." This comes in the form of a registration statement, a deep-dive into the company's finances and the bond's terms. It's designed to ensure investors aren't buying a mystery box.

These referees don't just watch the kickoff; they officiate the entire game. They set rules for how bonds are traded, fighting insider trading and market manipulation to ensure a fair and orderly market for everyone. Specialized markets have their own refs, too. The Municipal Securities Rulemaking Board (MSRB), for instance, sets the rules for bonds issued by cities and states, ensuring that this unique corner of the market is also safe and sound.

The Taxman's Toll: What You Actually Keep

After all is said and done, the taxman cometh. Tax considerations can dramatically change a bond's story. For most corporate and Treasury bonds, the interest you receive is taxable. Uncle Sam will want his share, and often your state will, too.

But there's a VIP section in the bond world: municipal bonds. The interest income from these "munis" is typically exempt from federal income tax. If you live in the state that issued the bond, it might be free from state and local taxes, too—a "triple-tax-exempt" prize. For someone in a high tax bracket, a muni yielding 3.5% could put more cash in their pocket than a corporate bond yielding 5% after the taxman takes his cut. This tax advantage makes munis the darling of high-income investors.

Don't forget about capital gains. If you sell a bond for more than you paid, the government wants to share in your success. Sell it for a loss, and the government will share a small piece of your pain by letting you deduct that loss.

And finally, beware of "phantom income." This is the bizarre tax headache that comes with zero-coupon bonds. Even though you receive no cash until the bond matures years from now, the IRS requires you to pay taxes on the interest it theoretically accrues each year. It's a tax bill for money you haven't yet seen—a crucial detail for any investor to plan around.

Fixed-Income Issuance and Trading

Beyond the bright lights and frantic energy of the stock market lies another financial universe—a vast, deep, and powerful ocean known as fixed income. While equities get the headlines, this is the world that provides the global economy's true ballast. It's the engine room, not the flashy bridge; the silent, powerful current, not the crashing waves. This is where promises are made, trust is priced, and the future is funded, one loan at a time. To understand it is to understand the very plumbing of our financial lives.

The Ecosystem of Lenders and Borrowers

Imagine the fixed-income world as a sprawling landscape populated by distinct tribes, each with its own culture, currency, and purpose. They are all connected by one thing: the art of the promise, the solemn vow to repay a debt.

The Bedrock: Government Bonds

This is the foundational layer of the entire system, built on the most powerful promise of all: that of a nation.

Issuers: Think of national governments as the ultimate borrowers. When the U.S. government issues a Treasury bond, it's not just raising money; it's borrowing against its full faith and credit, a promise so solid it's considered the global benchmark for safety. Closer to home, state and municipal governments ("munis") borrow to build the tangible world around us—the schools where our children learn, the bridges we cross, the water systems we rely on. In the U.S., these local promises often come with a unique perk: the interest you earn is tax-free, a quiet reward for investing in your own community.

Investors: Who buys these promises? Everyone seeking absolute stability. Central banks hold them as the core of their reserves. Pension funds and insurance companies, the guardians of our collective future, rely on their steady, predictable income to pay retirees and policyholders for decades to come. For them, a government bond isn't just an investment; it's a guarantee delivered.

The Engines of Commerce: Corporate Bonds

Here, the promises are made by the world's great enterprises, borrowing to fuel their ambitions, fund innovation, and build empires. This world is a spectrum of risk and reward.

Issuers: On one end, you have the blue-chip titans—companies with fortress-like balance sheets and sterling credit ratings (Investment-Grade). Their bonds are the reliable workhorses of the corporate world. On the other end, you have the daring, the recovering, or the up-and-coming—companies whose futures are less certain. Their High-Yield (or "junk") bonds are a high-stakes bet, offering tantalizingly high interest payments as compensation for the risk that the promise might be broken.

Investors: This segment attracts a different crowd. Asset managers and hedge funds are financial detectives, constantly searching for mispriced risk and opportunity. Pension funds dip into the safer, investment-grade waters for a bit more income. And specialized mutual funds act as tour guides, allowing everyday investors to explore this complex landscape, from the safest harbors to the most adventurous frontiers.

The Alchemists: Securitized Bonds

This is the most inventive, and at times controversial, corner of the fixed-income world. Here, financial engineers perform a kind of alchemy, transforming everyday debts into entirely new instruments.

The Process: Imagine thousands of individual promises—mortgage payments from homeowners, car loan payments, credit card bills—being gathered into a single, massive pool. This pool is then sliced and diced into new securities, which are sold to investors. A Mortgage-Backed Security (MBS) is a share in the payments of thousands of homeowners. An Asset-Backed Security (ABS) could be a claim on the revenue from a sea of auto loans.

The Players: This is a world for specialists. Investment banks act as the alchemists, sponsoring the creation of these complex structures. Hedge funds and other sophisticated institutions are drawn to the intricate risk-and-return profiles, while even central banks may buy them to help stabilize the housing market.

The Market's Pulse: Money Market Instruments

This is the high-speed, short-term heartbeat of the financial system. With maturities of a year or less, these instruments are less about long-term investment and more about managing the daily flow of cash. Think of them as the economy's checking account—safe, liquid, and essential for keeping the gears of commerce turning smoothly. Governments issue T-Bills, corporations issue Commercial Paper, and banks issue Certificates of Deposit (CDs), all to manage their cash needs for the immediate future.

Charting the Waters: The World of Indexes

How do you map such a vast and varied ocean? With fixed-income indexes. Far more than a simple list, these are sophisticated navigational charts that tell us where the market is, where it's been, and where the currents might be heading.

The Global Satellite View: Broad market indexes like the Bloomberg Global Aggregate are like a satellite image of the entire bond world, capturing thousands of government and corporate promises from dozens of countries. They give the most complete picture of the market's overall health.

Specialized Regional Maps: Other indexes zoom in. There are charts that map only the territory of U.S. Treasuries, others that focus exclusively on the landscape of European corporate debt, and still others that detail the terrain of emerging markets, where higher risks and rewards await.

Thematic Charts: Need to navigate a specific challenge? An Inflation-Linked Bond Index is a chart designed for stormy, inflationary weather, tracking bonds that protect your investment from rising prices. A High-Yield Index is a treasure map to the riskiest, but potentially most lucrative, part of the corporate world.

These indexes are not just for observation; they are the blueprints for countless ETFs and mutual funds, allowing investors to buy a slice of an entire market with a single click.

A Tale of Two Markets: Fixed Income vs. Equity

While they both exist to connect those who need capital with those who have it, the worlds of bonds and stocks operate on fundamentally different philosophies.

The Launch: Primary Markets

This is where securities are born.

An Equity IPO is a debutante ball. It's a public spectacle filled with hype, roadshows, and media coverage. Investors are buying a story, a piece of a dream, a share in the potential for future growth.

A Bond Issuance is a quiet, serious negotiation. It's often done behind closed doors between an issuer and a handful of large institutions. The focus isn't on dreams; it's on the cold, hard math of creditworthiness and the certainty of repayment. One is selling a vision; the other is signing a contract.

The Aftermarket: Secondary Markets

This is where securities live out their lives, traded between investors.

The Equity Market is a bustling, centralized bazaar like the New York Stock Exchange. Trading is transparent, with prices and volumes displayed for all to see in real-time. It's a standardized, high-energy environment.

The Bond Market is a sprawling, decentralized network. Most trading happens Over-the-Counter (OTC), in a web of dealers connected by phones and computer terminals. It's a world built on relationships and negotiation. Finding a buyer or seller for a specific, obscure bond can be like searching for a rare artifact, making it far less liquid and transparent than the stock market.

Ultimately, the two worlds reflect two different human desires. The equity investor is often a speculator, betting on capital appreciation and the thrill of growth. The fixed-income investor is typically a creditor, seeking the security of a predictable income stream and the return of their capital, not just a return on it. One is a ticket to the game; the other is a seat in the owner's box—less thrilling, perhaps, but with a contractual right to get paid.

Fixed-Income Markets for Corporate Issuers

The Financial Lifeblood: A Guide to Corporate Cash Flow

Think of the world of finance not as a cold ledger of numbers, but as a living, breathing ecosystem. In this world, money is like water—it must flow. Stagnant pools are useless, but a constant, managed current can power great enterprises. For any company, from a fledgling startup to a global titan, mastering the flow of cash is the difference between thriving and merely surviving. This is the art of funding, a tale told in two parts: the daily hustle for immediate cash and the epic quest for long-term capital.

The Daily Hustle: Your Short-Term Cash Playbook

Every business faces a relentless daily rhythm. Payroll is due, suppliers need to be paid, and sudden opportunities—or emergencies—can appear without warning. This is where the short-term funding toolkit comes in, offering a variety of ways to find cash in a pinch.

The Handshake Deal: Commercial Paper (CP)

Imagine the most exclusive club in the corporate world. The members are blue-chip companies with sterling reputations. Here, borrowing money doesn't require collateral or lengthy negotiations; it's done with a simple, trusted IOU. This is commercial paper. A respected corporation essentially says, "I need cash for a few months to stock my shelves for the holidays, and I'll pay you back with a little extra." Investors, like money market funds, line up to lend, confident in the company's promise. It's the financial equivalent of a firm handshake—fast, efficient, and built entirely on a foundation of trust and a pristine track record.

The Trusted Advisor: Bank Loans & Lines of Credit

Not everyone is in that exclusive club. For most companies, the bank is a vital partner. Securing a line of credit is like having a trusted advisor who's given you a key to a vault. You don't have to use it, but you sleep better knowing that if a sudden storm hits—say, the price of raw materials skyrockets—you can unlock the funds you need to ride it out. It's a relationship, not just a transaction. The bank knows your story, your struggles, and your potential, offering a flexible lifeline that's more personal and accessible than the open market.

The Global Passport: Bankers' Acceptances (BAs)

Picture an American coffee roaster trying to buy a unique harvest from a small farm in Colombia. The farmer has never heard of the roaster, and the roaster is hesitant to send cash to a stranger across the globe. How do you build trust where there is none? You bring in a referee: the bank. A Banker's Acceptance is like a financial passport. The roaster's bank stamps its guarantee on the deal, promising to pay the Colombian farmer on a set date. The farmer is assured payment, and the roaster gets the beans, with time to sell them before the bill comes due. The bank's guarantee transforms a risky international deal into a rock-solid, tradable instrument, oiling the gears of global commerce.

The Banks' Secret Handshake: The Federal Funds Market

After the markets close, there's a secret, high-speed marketplace just for banks. This is the federal funds market. Imagine one bank ending the day with a bit too much cash in its vault to meet regulations, while another is just a little short. Instead of sounding alarms, they engage in a simple, overnight loan. The bank with extra cash lends to the bank in need at the federal funds rate. It's the unseen plumbing of the financial system, a quiet, efficient mechanism that ensures every institution is stable and the entire network runs without a single hiccup.

A Deeper Dive: The Financial Pawn Shop for the Powerful

Among these tools, one stands out for its sheer scale and cleverness: the repurchase agreement, or repo. Don't let the technical name fool you. At its heart, a repo is the most sophisticated pawn shop in the world.

Instead of a vintage guitar or a diamond ring, the collateral here is a pile of ultra-safe government bonds. A bank or a large fund needs cash—fast. They "sell" their bonds to an investor with an ironclad promise to buy them back tomorrow, or next week, at a slightly higher price. That small price difference is the interest paid for the loan.

The seller gets instant cash to navigate the day, without having to permanently part with their best assets. The buyer (the lender) gets to park their idle cash in an incredibly safe, short-term investment, secured by the best collateral on earth. It's a brilliant win-win. Central banks, like the Federal Reserve, even use repos as their primary tool to inject or drain cash from the entire banking system, effectively setting the pulse for the nation's economy.

But even in this high-end pawn shop, there are risks. What if the "pawned" collateral suddenly loses value? What if the counterparty—the other side of your deal—goes bust overnight? To protect against this, lenders often demand a "haircut," lending slightly less than the collateral's full market value. It's a small buffer, a safety net in a world that moves at the speed of light.

Building an Empire: The Great Divide in Long-Term Funding

While short-term funding is about surviving the day, long-term funding is about building a legacy. It's the capital needed to build new factories, launch revolutionary products, and expand across the globe. Here, the corporate world splits into two vastly different realms: the kingdom of the investment-grade aristocrats and the rugged frontier of the high-yield pioneers.

The Aristocrats: Investment-Grade Issuers

These are the blue-bloods of the business world—companies with fortress-like balance sheets, predictable profits, and names that inspire confidence. When they need to raise money for the long haul, the capital markets roll out the red carpet. They issue corporate bonds at whisper-low interest rates because investors see them as a sure thing. Pension funds and insurance companies clamor to lend them money, seeking safety and stability. For these companies, raising billions is a smooth, dignified affair. The rules are few, the costs are low, and the world is their oyster. They have the financial firepower to dream big and build empires that last for generations.

The Pioneers & The Comeback Kids: High-Yield Issuers

On the other side of the tracks live the high-yield issuers. These aren't bad companies; they are the bold, the ambitious, the misunderstood. They might be a young tech firm with a disruptive idea but no profits yet, or an older company in a tough industry fighting its way back to glory. They are often called "junk" issuers, but that's unfair. They are simply riskier.

When these pioneers need to raise money, they can't whisper; they have to shout. They issue high-yield bonds, promising much higher returns to lure investors willing to take a gamble. These investors are financial adventurers, betting on a turnaround story or a breakthrough innovation, hoping for a handsome reward for their courage. For the high-yield company, this capital comes at a cost. The interest rates are steep, and the loan agreements are often loaded with "covenants"—strict rules that can feel like a financial straightjacket, limiting their freedom to maneuver. For them, every dollar raised is a hard-won victory, fuel for a riskier but potentially more thrilling journey.

In the end, the world of funding is a reflection of the human drama of ambition, risk, and reputation. From the quick, daily transactions that keep the lights on to the massive, long-term bets that shape our future, finance is the powerful current that connects us all, driving the engine of progress and innovation.

Fixed-Income Markets for Government Issuers

The Financial Heartbeat of Nations and Neighbors

Sovereign Governments: The Architects of Economies

A nation's government is like a master architect with a sprawling blueprint for society. To build the roads, schools, and hospitals—and to stand guard over it all—it needs a vast quarry of resources. Its primary tool is taxation, the lifeblood drawn from the economic activity of its people and businesses. This is the steady, rhythmic income that keeps the lights on and the country running.

But when a nation dreams bigger than its annual income—to launch a massive infrastructure project or navigate a sudden crisis—it turns to the art of borrowing. It makes promises in the form of debt. These aren't all the same; they're a spectrum of vows made to the future.

The Short-Term Handshake (T–Bills): Think of these as quick, informal loans from the market, promised to be repaid in a year or less. They are a government's tool for managing its daily cash flow, a way to smooth out the lumpy rhythm of income and expenses.

The Mid-Term Pledge (T–Notes): Stretching out for up to a decade, these are the workhorses of government finance, funding the steady, ongoing work of the nation.

The Generational Vow (T–Bonds): With timelines stretching thirty years or more, these are promises made by one generation to be honored by the next. They finance legacies—interstate highways, monumental research projects, and the long-term management of national debt.

The Inflation-Proof Promise (e.g., TIPS): In a world where the value of money can erode, these special bonds are a solemn guarantee that an investor's capital will not be silently eaten by inflation.

Sometimes, a nation sells off family heirlooms through privatization—turning state-owned companies over to private hands for a huge, one-time infusion of cash. And then there is seigniorage, the quiet magic of the mint. It's the profit made simply by printing a dollar for pennies, a subtle power that, if overused, can unleash the destructive ghost of inflation.

Non-Sovereign Governments: The Community Builders

State, provincial, and city governments are the builders we see every day. Their financial world is more intimate, their resources more constrained. They thrive on local taxes—the property taxes that fund the neighborhood school, the sales taxes that pay for the fire department. Their work is tangible, its funding rooted in the community it serves.

They often look to the central government for grants, like a regional office receiving its budget from headquarters. But to build a new library or bridge, they also enter the world of borrowing by issuing municipal bonds. A "muni" bond is a pact with investors, a promise to build something for the public good. Often, this promise comes with a sweetener: the interest earned is tax-free, a feature that makes them a quiet favorite among savvy investors.

Quasi-Government Entities: The Financial Hybrids

Imagine an entity with the body of a private company but the soul of a public servant. These are the quasi-government organizations, like America's Fannie Mae and Freddie Mac. They are created to serve a public mission—in this case, to keep the river of money flowing into the home mortgage market. They don't tax or print money. Instead, they issue their own debt, which the market views as exceptionally safe because of an unspoken, implicit guarantee from the government. They are the market's hidden plumbing, ensuring that vital social and economic goals have a steady financial current, all thanks to that powerful government wink.

Supranational Agencies: The Global Financial Arbiters

Entities like the World Bank and the International Monetary Fund (IMF) exist on a plane above individual nations. They are the financial architects of the global order. Their funding begins with capital contributions from their member countries, nations pooling their strength to create something more powerful than any single state.

With this collective backing, they step into the global capital markets and borrow immense sums at the lowest possible rates—their credit is, after all, backed by the entire world. They then turn around and act as a combination of a global development bank and an economic emergency room, lending these funds to nations for transformative projects or to stabilize a teetering economy. They are part bank, part diplomat, wielding finance as a tool for global progress and stability.

A Tale of Two Bonds: The People's Promise vs. The Innovator's Gamble

At their core, all bonds are promises. But a bond born from the full faith of a nation and one born from the ambition of a corporation lead very different lives.

The Government Bond: A Birthright of Trust

A government bond is born not in a quiet office, but in a grand, public ceremony—an auction. It is an event of supreme transparency and predictability. The government announces its needs, and a special class of financial institutions, the primary dealers, are obligated to show up and bid, ensuring the promise is funded. Its birth is a matter of public record, its size titanic.

From the moment it enters the world, this bond lives in a vast, deep ocean of liquidity. The market for U.S. Treasuries is the most liquid on Earth. It can be traded in milliseconds, its price a globally recognized signal of economic health. It isn't just a loan; it's the benchmark, the "risk-free" North Star by which all other financial instruments in that currency navigate. Its life is one of stability and authority. It is the bedrock.

The Corporate Bond: A Tailored Ambition

A corporate bond's birth is a more bespoke affair. It is crafted in the design studios of investment banks, an act of underwriting where the bank acts as a sponsor, introducing this new promise to the investing world. It doesn't have the inherent trust of a nation; it must earn it. Its pedigree is examined by rating agencies—the Moody's and S&P's of the world—who act as judges, assigning it a grade that will define its life.

Unlike the standardized government bond, a corporate bond is a chameleon. It can be callable, giving its issuer the right to pay it back early. It can be convertible, carrying a secret dream of one day becoming a share of the company's stock. It might be born in a public offering or through a private placement, a quiet pact made with a handful of large institutions.

Its life after birth is more complex. The market is not one deep ocean but a galaxy of smaller, less connected pools. Liquidity can be thin. Finding a buyer or seller for a specific bond from a mid-sized company can be a search, not a certainty. Its value is tethered to a single story: the quarterly earnings, the new product launch, the scandal in the boardroom. Trading this bond requires not just faith, but constant vigilance and deep analysis of the company's fate. It carries more risk, but in that risk lies the potential for a greater reward. It is not the bedrock, but the dynamic, ever-changing skyline built upon it.

Fixed-Income Bond Valuation: Prices and Yields

The Secret Life of a Bond's Price: What You Actually Pay

So, you're thinking about buying a bond. Awesome! Most people think of a bond's price as this one, solid number. But the truth is a little more interesting, especially if you're not buying it on its birthday (a coupon payment date).

Imagine you're buying a rental property. The seller has been collecting rent all month. If you buy it on the 15th, it's only fair that you pay the seller for the 15 days of rent they've already "earned" but haven't collected yet, right?

Bonds work the exact same way.

The Clean Price: This is like the agreed-upon price of the house itself. It's the number you see quoted everywhere. It's a clean, simple value based on all the future payments the bond will make, discounted to today's value.

Accrued Interest: This is that pro-rated rent. The seller owned the bond for, say, 45 days since the last coupon payment. They've earned 45 days' worth of interest, and you, the buyer, have to pay them for it. It's calculated simply:

AccruedInterest=(CouponPayment)×TotaldaysincouponperiodDayssincelastcoupon

The Dirty Price (or Full Price): This is the final, all-in price you actually hand over. It's the sticker price of the house plus that pro-rated rent.

Dirty Price = Clean Price + Accrued Interest

When you buy a bond on a coupon date, the accrued interest is zero, so the clean and dirty prices are the same. But since most trades happen between these dates, this little bit of "rental math" ensures everyone gets their fair share.

The Dance of the Bond Variables: A Four-Way Relationship

A bond's price isn't set in a vacuum. It's in a constant dance with three other key players: its coupon rate, its maturity, and the market's yield-to-maturity (YTM). Understanding this dance is the key to mastering bonds.

1. The Seesaw: Price vs. Yield (YTM) ⚖️

This is the big one. A bond's price and its YTM have an inverse relationship. Think of them on a seesaw.

When the market's interest rates (YTM) go up, the bond's price goes down.

When the market's interest rates (YTM) go down, the bond's price goes up.

Why? Imagine you own a bond that pays a 3% coupon. Suddenly, new bonds with the same risk are being issued that pay 5% (the YTM has risen). Your 3% bond looks pretty lame now, doesn't it? To make it attractive to a buyer, you have to sell it for a lower price to make up for its lower payments.

2. The Sprinkles: Price vs. Coupon Rate 🍩

This one's easy: More is more. Holding everything else constant, a bond with a higher coupon rate will have a higher price. It's just more valuable because it pays you more cash. An 8% coupon bond is simply a tastier treat than a 4% coupon bond, so you'll pay more for it.

3. The Drama Queen: Price vs. Maturity 🎭

The longer a bond's maturity, the more sensitive and dramatic its price is to changes in interest rates. A 30-year bond will see its price swing wildly with a 1% change in market rates, while a 2-year bond will barely flinch.

Think of it like a long-term relationship versus a short-term one. Small bumps in the road have a much bigger impact when you're committed for 30 years. This heightened sensitivity to interest rate changes is known as interest rate risk.

4. The Report Card: YTM vs. Coupon Rate 🎓

This relationship tells you if a bond is an A-student, a C-student, or just average. It determines if the bond sells for more, less, or exactly its face value.

Premium Bond (A+): If your bond's Coupon Rate > YTM, it's a star performer. It pays more than the current market rate. Investors will pay a premium (a price higher than its face value) to own it.

Discount Bond (C-): If your bond's Coupon Rate < YTM, it's an underperformer. It pays less than the market rate. To attract buyers, it must sell at a discount (a price lower than its face value).

Par Bond (B): If your bond's Coupon Rate = YTM, it's perfectly average. It pays exactly what the market expects. It will trade at par (its price is its face value).

Matrix Pricing: The Art of Financial Detective Work 🕵️

What happens when you need to price a bond that's so rare it almost never trades? There's no recent "last sold" price to look at. Is it just a guessing game? Not quite. Welcome to matrix pricing.

Think of it like trying to price a unique, custom-built house in a neighborhood with no identical homes. How would a real estate agent do it? They wouldn't just throw up their hands. They'd become a detective.

They'd look for comparable houses that have sold recently. They'd find homes with:

A similar location and quality (Credit Rating)

A similar age (Maturity)

A similar number of bedrooms (Coupon Rate)

Similar features, like a pool or finished basement (Callability/Putability Features)

Once they have data on a few similar-but-not-identical houses, they can make a highly educated guess. If a 3-bedroom sold for $400k and a 5-bedroom sold for $600k, they can logically infer that our custom 4-bedroom house is probably worth somewhere around $500k.

That's exactly what matrix pricing does for bonds.

The Detective's Process:

Profile the Target: First, you identify all the key features of your mysterious, illiquid bond (its credit rating, maturity date, coupon, etc.).

Find the "Comps": You scour the market for actively traded bonds that are as similar as possible to your target. You're looking for bonds with the same credit rating and a range of maturities that bracket your bond's maturity.

Build the Matrix: You organize the yields of these comparable bonds into a grid or a simple yield curve. For example, you might see that all AA-rated industrial bonds maturing in 5 years yield 4.1%, while those maturing in 10 years yield 4.6%.

Connect the Dots (Interpolate): Your mystery bond matures in 7 years. Using the matrix, you can interpolate—find the point in between the 5-year and 10-year yields—to estimate that your 7-year bond should have a yield of around 4.3%.

Price It! With this estimated yield, you can now plug it into the standard bond pricing formula to calculate the bond's fair price.

Matrix pricing isn't a perfect science—it's a sophisticated estimation. Its accuracy depends entirely on how good your "comps" are. But in the murky world of thinly traded securities, it's an indispensable tool that brings logic and order to the challenge of pricing the unpriceable.

Yield and Yield Spread Measures for Fixed-Rate Bonds

Part 1: The Secret Sauce of Compounding: Why a Bond's Payout Schedule Matters

Think of a bond's interest rate—its coupon—as a promise. A company promises to pay you 5% a year for loaning them your money. But the real magic isn't just in what they promise, but in how often they deliver on it. This is the secret sauce of investing: compounding.

Imagine you're building a snowball. The "nominal yield" is the handful of snow you start with. If the company pays you just once a year, you get to roll that snowball just once. It gets a little bigger.

But what if they paid you twice a year?

That's semi-annual compounding. After six months, they hand you a small payment. It's not just money in your pocket; it's a new layer of snow for your ball. For the next six months, you aren't just earning interest on your original investment, you're earning interest on your interest. Your snowball is picking up more snow, faster.

Let's put some numbers to this snowball effect, using a simple $1,000 bond with a 5% nominal rate.

Annual Payout (One Big Payday): You get $50 at the end of the year. Your true return, or Effective Annual Yield (EAY), is exactly 5%. Simple.

Semi-Annual Payouts (Two Smaller Paydays): You receive $25 every six months. After the first payment, that

$25 can start working for you. This tiny head start bumps your true return up.

The math looks like this: $EAY=(1+20.05)2-1$.

This gives you an EAY of 5.06%. It's not a fortune, but it's free money, earned simply because your payouts were more frequent.

Quarterly Payouts (Four Little Paydays): Now you're getting paid every three months. Each payment is smaller, but it gets to work for you even sooner. Your snowball gets rolled four times a year.

The math: $EAY=(1+40.05)4-1$.

Your EAY climbs to 5.09%.

Monthly Payouts (Twelve Tiny Paydays): With monthly payments, your money is constantly being put back to work.

The math: $EAY=(1+120.05)12-1$.

Your EAY nudges up to 5.12%.

The Big Idea: The more frequently a bond pays you, the harder your money works. The nominal rate is the sticker price, but the Effective Annual Yield (EAY) is your true take-home return. When comparing two bonds with the same coupon rate, the one that pays out more often is giving you a slightly better deal. It's a small detail that reveals a powerful truth about how wealth is built: not just in lump sums, but in steady, compounding streams.

Part 2: Decoding a Bond's True Story: A Guide to Yields and Spreads

A bond's coupon rate is just the cover of the book. It's the first thing you see, but it hardly tells the whole story. To truly understand a bond's value and its place in your portfolio, you need to read the chapters inside. These chapters are written in the language of yields and spreads.

The Different "Chapters" of Yield

Each yield measure tells you something different about the bond's potential return.

The "Right-Now" Yield (Current Yield):
This is the most straightforward measure. It asks: "Based on what I pay for this bond today, what is its annual income return?"

Calculation: Current Yield = Annual Interest Payment / Current Market Price

The Story It Tells: Imagine a bond that pays $50 a year is on sale for $950. Its Current Yield is $50 / $950, or 5.26%. This is a useful snapshot for income seekers. But it's just that—a snapshot. It completely ignores what happens when the bond matures.

The "Full Story" Yield (Yield to Maturity - YTM):
This is the most important chapter. YTM tells you the total return you'll get if you buy the bond today and hold it all the way to the end. It accounts for every coupon payment and the final principal repayment.

The Story It Tells: YTM is like a movie spoiler—it tells you how it all ends.

If YTM is higher than the coupon rate, it means the bond is selling at a discount (like our $950 bond). You get the bonus of buying cheap and being paid back the full face value at the end.

If YTM is lower than the coupon rate, the bond is selling at a premium. You're paying extra for a higher income stream, so your total return is slightly lower.

YTM is the closest thing we have to a bond's "true" long-term return.

The "Plot Twist" Yield (Yield to Call - YTC):
Some bonds have a plot twist: a "call feature." This gives the issuer the right to buy the bond back from you early (usually when interest rates have fallen).

The Story It Tells: YTC calculates your return if the story gets cut short. If you buy a bond that's likely to be called, the YTC is a far more realistic number than the YTM. It's the cautious investor's guide to what they can actually expect.

Spreads: The Price Tag for Risk

Spreads measure the gap between a bond's yield and a super-safe benchmark, like a U.S. Treasury bond. Think of a spread as the extra payment you demand for taking on extra risk. It's the market's price tag for danger.

The Basic Risk Thermometer (Benchmark Spread or G-Spread):
This is the simplest spread. It's the difference between your bond's yield and a government bond of the same maturity.

Example: A corporate bond yields 6%, and a Treasury bond yields 4%. The spread is 2%, or 200 basis points (bps).

The Story It Tells: That 200 bps is your compensation for choosing the corporate bond over the risk-free Treasury. When investors are nervous, they demand more compensation, and spreads widen. When they're confident, spreads narrow.

The Pro-Level Gauges (Z-Spread and OAS):
These are more sophisticated tools for a more precise reading.

Z-Spread (Zero-Volatility Spread): Instead of comparing your bond to a single Treasury, the Z-Spread compares it to the entire government yield curve. It's a more accurate, holistic measure of the risk premium across the bond's whole life.

OAS (Option-Adjusted Spread): This is the X-ray machine for bonds with those tricky plot twists (like call features). It cleverly calculates the value of that option and strips it out, showing you the "pure" spread you're earning for the credit risk alone. It answers the question: "Setting aside any funny business with call options, how much am I really getting paid for the risk that this company might not pay me back?"

Why Read the Whole Book?

Understanding these measures moves you from being a passive bond holder to an active, informed investor. They are the tools that allow you to look past the cover and see the real story. By comparing yields and tracking spreads, you can assess risk, spot value, and build a fixed-income portfolio that is resilient, robust, and truly aligned with your financial goals.

Yield and Yield Spread Measures for Floating-Rate Instruments

The Secret Language of Yields: A Guide to Floating-Rate and Money Market Instruments

In the vast universe of finance, some instruments are like steady, predictable planets, orbiting with fixed paths. Others are more like comets, their brightness and trajectory shifting with the gravitational pull of the market. This guide is about decoding the language of these more dynamic instruments: the adaptable floating-rate notes and the fast-moving money market securities. Understanding their yields isn't just about crunching numbers; it's about learning to read the story they tell about risk, reward, and the true value of money.

Part 1: The Pulse of the Market - Yield Spreads for Floating-Rate Instruments

Imagine a ship whose sails automatically trim themselves to the prevailing winds. That's a floating-rate instrument. Instead of a fixed interest payment, its coupon is a promise to pay a certain amount above a benchmark rate like SOFR. As the market's winds shift, so does the payout.

But how do you judge the value of such a fluid promise? You measure the "spread"—the extra reward you get for choosing this particular ship over the safe harbor of a benchmark. This spread isn't just a number; it's a narrative about the issuer's seaworthiness, the instrument's desirability, and any hidden currents in its contract.

a. The Fortune Teller: Discount Margin (DM)

The Discount Margin (DM) is the most holistic of these measures. Think of it as the instrument's true north, pointing toward the average extra return you can expect over its entire life. It's the magic number that perfectly balances the price you pay today with all the future (and fluctuating) cash you hope to receive.

The Story it Tells: The DM answers the essential question: "Considering the price I'm paying today (which might be more or less than face value), what is the real bonus I'm getting on top of the benchmark?" A high DM whispers of higher risk or a bargain to be had—the market is demanding more compensation. A low DM suggests a safe, blue-chip name that doesn't need to offer a big premium to attract investors. It's the market's collective wisdom about an instrument's future, distilled into a single number.

b. The Sticker Price: Quoted Margin (QM)

The Quoted Margin (QM) is the advertised bonus. If a floater's coupon is "SOFR + 75 basis points," the QM is simply 75 basis points (or 0.75%). It's the number written on the box, the official promise.

The Story it Tells: The QM is the starting point of the conversation, not the end. It's the contractual spread, clean and simple. But just like a car's sticker price, it doesn't tell you what the car is really worth on the open market. If investors are worried, they'll sell the instrument for less than its face value, meaning their actual return (the DM) will be higher than the QM. The QM is the promise; the DM is the reality.

c. The X-Ray Vision: Option-Adjusted Spread (OAS)

Some floating-rate instruments come with bells and whistles—embedded options like "caps" (a maximum payout) or "floors" (a minimum payout). These features are like secret clauses in the contract that can dramatically change the instrument's behavior. The Option-Adjusted Spread (OAS) is a powerful tool with X-ray vision, designed to see through these options and find the "pure" spread underneath.

The Story it Tells: The OAS isolates the compensation you're getting for credit and liquidity risk alone, stripping away the value of any embedded options. It answers, "If we ignore all the fancy features, what is the raw risk premium here?" This allows for a true apples-to-apples comparison. If two floaters have similar DMs, but one has a much higher OAS, it's a red flag. It means that after accounting for its options, that instrument is carrying a lot more fundamental risk for the same apparent return.

Part 2: The Financial System's High-Speed Rail - Yields for Money Market Instruments

Welcome to the money market, the financial system's circulatory system. This is where cash moves at lightning speed, in the form of short-term loans that last anywhere from a day to a year. Instruments like Treasury bills (T-bills) and commercial paper are the bedrock of this world.

Many of these are "discount" instruments. Think of it like buying a $100 gift card for $98. You don't receive periodic interest; your profit is the $2 difference you pocket when the card matures. Calculating the yield on this simple transaction, however, has its own unique quirks and dialects.

a. The Old-School Yardstick: Bank Discount Yield (BDY)

The Bank Discount Yield (BDY) is the traditional language of T-bills. It's a quick-and-dirty calculation that expresses the discount as a percentage of the face value and then annualizes it using a 360-day "banker's year."

The Story it Tells: The BDY is simple and conventional, but it's a bit of a funhouse mirror. By using the face value in the denominator, it understates your true return on the money you actually invested. And the 360-day year makes it hard to compare with almost anything else. It's a specialized dialect, useful only for speaking with others who use it.

Formula: BDY=Face ValueDiscount×Days to Maturity360

b. The Universal Translator: Bond Equivalent Yield (BEY)

The Bond Equivalent Yield (BEY) is the hero of comparability. It translates the quirky dialect of the BDY into the common language of the broader bond market. It corrects the BDY's two main flaws: it calculates the return based on the price you paid and uses a standard 365-day year.

The Story it Tells: The BEY provides a much more honest picture of your return, allowing you to compare a 90-day T-bill directly to a 2-year Treasury note. It levels the playing field, ensuring you're not tricked by the conventions of different markets.

Formula: BEY=Purchase PriceDiscount×Days to Maturity365

c. The Ultimate Truth: Effective Annual Yield (EAY)

The Effective Annual Yield (EAY) tells the whole story by revealing the power of compounding. It answers the most important question: "If I could reinvest this return at the same rate over and over, what would I truly earn in a full year?"

The Story it Tells: EAY is the gold standard for comparison. It accounts for the fact that earning 2% over three months is better than earning 8% over a year, because you get your money back faster and can put it to work again. It reveals the true growth potential of your investment, making it the most accurate measure of all.

Formula (Conceptual): EAY=(1+Periodic Rate)Number of Periods in a Year−1

Conclusion: From Numbers to Knowledge

Whether dissecting the subtle risk premiums in a floating-rate note or translating the arcane yields of a T-bill, these measures are more than just formulas. They are the analytical tools that transform raw data into financial wisdom. They allow us to look past the sticker price to see the true value, to peer through contractual fog to spot underlying risk, and to compare wildly different instruments on a level playing field. Mastering this language empowers us to make smarter decisions, manage risk more effectively, and ultimately, navigate the complex waters of the financial world with greater confidence and clarity.

The Term Structure of Interest Rates: Spot, Par, and Forward Curves

1. The Secret Language of Time and Money: Decoding Spot Rates

Imagine you could buy a single promise. Not a complex contract, just a simple, ironclad guarantee: you give someone money today, and on a specific date in the future, they give you a single, larger payment back. No interest checks along the way, no complications. Just one payment, one future date.

The interest rate that makes this deal fair is called a spot rate. It's the purest expression of the time value of money for that specific time horizon. Think of it as the "non-stop flight" of interest rates—a direct route from your investment today to your payoff tomorrow. It's the true, unadulterated yield for a single cash flow at a single point in the future.

Now, picture a whole constellation of these spot rates. One star represents the rate for a guaranteed payment in one year. Another, slightly farther away, represents the rate for a payment in two years, and so on, out to 30 years or more. If you connect these stars, you create a luminous map of the market's current financial landscape. This map is the spot curve (or the zero-coupon curve).

This curve doesn't just sit there; it tells a story. An upward-sloping curve, rising gently into the distance, whispers of optimism—the market believes the economy will grow, and it demands a higher return for locking up money for longer. But an inverted curve, sloping ominously downward, is like seeing storm clouds on the horizon. It suggests the market is bracing for an economic slowdown, with future rates expected to be lower than today's.

So, how does this help us price a real-world bond, with all its messy coupon payments?

This is where the magic of the spot curve shines. A traditional bond isn't a single promise; it's a bundle of promises. Each coupon payment is a small, individual promise, and the final principal repayment is one big promise. The spot curve allows us to treat them as such. Instead of using one blunt instrument (a single yield-to-maturity) to value the whole bundle, we use a set of precision tools. We take each promised cash flow and discount it to today's value using the specific spot rate that matches its exact maturity.

Let's watch this in action. Say we have a two-year bond with a $1,000 face value and a 5% annual coupon. The market tells us the one-year spot rate is 4% and the two-year spot rate is 4.5%.

Promise #1 (Year 1): A $50 coupon payment. We discount this using the one-year spot rate.
Present Value = $50 / (1 + 0.04)^1 = $48.08

Promise #2 (Year 2): A final $50 coupon plus the $1,000 principal, totaling $1,050. We discount this using the two-year spot rate.
Present Value = $1,050 / (1 + 0.045)^2 = $961.54

The true price of the bond is simply the sum of its time-traveled parts:

Bond Price = $48.08 + $961.54 = $1,009.62

By valuing each piece of the bond on its own terms, we arrive at a price that is far more precise and reflective of the market's true feelings about risk and time. The spot rate is the atomic unit of interest, the fundamental building block from which all other, more complex bond math is built.

2. The Market's Billboard and Its Weather Forecast: Par and Forward Rates

If spot rates are the hidden, fundamental particles of the interest rate universe, then par and forward rates are the more visible phenomena they create. They are the market's everyday language, translating the theoretical into the practical.

Par Rates: The Market's "Sticker Price"

Imagine walking into a bond marketplace and asking, "What coupon rate would make a brand-new, 10-year bond sell for exactly its face value today?" The answer to that question is the 10-year par rate. It's the yield-to-maturity of a bond trading "at par."

The collection of these par rates across different maturities forms the par curve. This is the curve you most often see on the evening news or in financial reports—it's the market's billboard, advertising the general yield for standard, coupon-paying government bonds. It's a blended, real-world rate, calculated by finding the coupon that makes a bond's price (when discounted by the more fundamental spot rates) equal its face value.

The formula for the par coupon rate (CN) for a bond with N years to maturity looks complex, but its soul is simple: it finds the single coupon rate that balances the equation.
CN=Σi=1N(1+Si)i1 1−(1+SN)N1

Here, S_i is the spot rate for each year i. This formula is essentially solving for the coupon that makes the present value of all cash flows equal to the bond's face value.

Forward Rates: The Financial Weather Forecast

Now for the most intriguing concept: the forward rate. A forward rate is the market's ghost in the machine. It's an interest rate for a future period that is implied by today's spot rates. Think of it as locking in a loan rate today for a loan that starts one year from now. It answers the question: "Based on today's two-year and one-year rates, what does the market believe the one-year interest rate will be, one year from today?"

This isn't just guesswork; it's a mathematical necessity to prevent risk-free profits. The market is telling us that you should be indifferent between two choices:

Investing for two years at the two-year spot rate (S_2).

Investing for one year at the one-year spot rate (S_1) and simultaneously locking in a rate to reinvest for the second year (the forward rate, $f_{1,1}$).

The math that connects them is elegant:

$$(1+S_2)^2=(1+S_1)^1\times(1+f_{1,1})^1$$

From this, we can solve for the forward rate, the market's "weather forecast" for interest rates. Conversely, we can build the entire spot curve from a series of these one-period forward rates, like building a long bridge one section at a time. The two-year spot rate is just the geometric average of the forward rate from year 0 to 1 and the forward rate from year 1 to 2.

$$(1+S_N)^N=(1+f_{0,1})(1+f_{1,1})\ldots(1+f_{N-1,1})$$

While you can price a bond by discounting its cash flows back to the present one year at a time using this chain of forward rates, it's more of a conceptual exercise. Its true value is in what it reveals: the market's embedded expectations about the future path of interest rates, which is vital for everything from corporate planning to derivative pricing.

3. A Tale of Three Curves: Spot, Par, and Forward

Imagine three experts are asked to describe the same landscape—the term structure of interest rates. Each uses a different lens, giving a unique yet related perspective. These are our three curves.

The Spot Curve: The Pure Theorist
The spot curve is the bedrock, the most fundamental truth. Each point on this curve represents the pure, unadulterated interest rate for a single cash payment at a single point in the future. It's a theoretical construct, often bootstrapped from market prices, but it's the engine of valuation. When you want the most accurate price for any stream of cash flows, you turn to the theorist's spot curve. It's the DNA of the term structure.

The Par Curve: The Market Populist
The par curve is the face of the market. It's the one you see quoted everywhere because it represents the yields of familiar, coupon-paying bonds that are trading at face value. It's directly observable and easily understood. However, it's a blended rate, an average. The yield on a 10-year par bond is a mix of ten different spot rates discounting its coupons and principal. It tells a great story about the market's general mood, but it lacks the precision of the spot curve for valuing unique cash flows.

The Forward Curve: The Fortune Teller

The forward curve is the most dynamic and speculative of the three. It's a map of the market's implied predictions. It tells you what the market expects a one-year interest rate to be, five years from now. It is derived from the spot curve and reflects the collective wisdom (or folly) of traders about future economic policy, inflation, and growth. An upward-sloping forward curve is the market shouting, "We think rates are going up!" It is the leading indicator, revealing the momentum baked into the system.

The Dance of the Curves

These three curves don't exist in isolation; they are locked in a mathematical dance dictated by the law of no-arbitrage. Their relationship reveals deeper truths:

When the spot curve is rising, the par curve will lie just below it. Why? The coupons of a long-term par bond get discounted by the earlier, lower spot rates, which drags its overall yield (the par rate) down. The forward curve, in this case, will soar above both. For the average rate (the spot rate) to be pulled up, the future rates (the forward rates) must be significantly higher.

When the spot curve is falling (inverted), the roles reverse. The par curve will ride above the spot curve, as the earlier, higher spot rates give more weight to the coupons. The forward curve will dive below both, signaling the market's expectation of future rate cuts.

If the spot curve were perfectly flat, all three curves would merge into a single, straight line—a rare moment of perfect equilibrium in expectations and reality.

In essence, the spot curve tells us the price of money now. The par curve gives us a practical, observable summary for the bonds we trade every day. And the forward curve whispers to us about the price of money tomorrow. Together, they provide a rich, three-dimensional view of the ever-shifting world of interest rates.

Interest Rate Risk and Return

The Secret Symphony of a Bond: More Than a Simple Note

Think of a bond not as a sterile contract, but as a living piece of music. You, the investor, are the conductor. Buying a bond seems simple: you hand over your money, and in return, you get a promise of a steady rhythm of payments. But a true maestro knows the final performance is far more than just the melody written on the page. It's a symphony of three distinct movements, each contributing to the rich, final sound of your total return.

The First Movement: The Unwavering Melody (Coupon Payments)

This is the part of the music everyone hears first. The coupon payments are the clear, predictable melody of your investment. If you own a $1,000 bond with a 5% coupon, you are promised a crisp $50 note played for you each year. This steady beat is the heart of the bond's appeal—a reliable rhythm section in the often-chaotic orchestra of the market. For the investor who simply wants to buy the sheet music, sit back, and listen until the final note (maturity), this melody, combined with the grand finale of getting their principal back, is the core of the composition. It's the beautiful, simple tune you signed up for.

The Second Movement: The Echoes You Create (Reinvestment Income)

Here's where you, the conductor, start to add your own artistry. When that $50 coupon payment arrives, it doesn't just fade into silence. You have a choice. Do you let it disappear, or do you reinvest it? When you reinvest that coupon, it begins to create its own music—its own echoes of interest. This is your reinvestment income.

This movement introduces a fascinating improvisation. If the concert hall (the market) has become more vibrant and interest rates have risen, your reinvested coupons can be put to work at a higher tempo, earning more and amplifying your total return. If rates have fallen, the echoes will be softer, potentially quieting your overall performance. This is the snowball effect in musical form; the echoes build upon themselves, and their power over time can be astonishingly profound, transforming a simple melody into a complex, layered harmony.

The Third Movement: The Roar of the Crowd (Capital Gains or Losses)

This final movement only plays if you decide to end the concert early by selling your bond. The value of your bond isn't just what's written on the sheet music; it's also about how much the audience (the market) wants to hear your particular song right now.

Imagine you bought your bond when its 5% melody was standard. Now, newly written songs (new bonds) are only offering a 3% tune. Suddenly, your 5% classic is a coveted hit! The crowd will pay a premium to hear it, and if you sell, you walk away with a capital gain—the financial equivalent of a standing ovation.

Conversely, if new bonds are being issued with a dazzling 7% melody, your 5% tune seems a bit dated. To get someone to take your ticket, you'll have to offer it at a discount, resulting in a capital loss. This movement is driven by the shifting mood of the market, and it can add a dramatic crescendo of profit or a somber diminuendo of loss to your bond's story.

The Tightrope Walk: Duration, Your Horizon, and the Art of Balance

Now, let's take these musical concepts and place them on a stage. Imagine yourself as a tightrope walker. Your goal is to get to the other side of a canyon. This journey represents your bond investment.

Your Destination (The Investment Horizon): The platform you're walking toward is your investment horizon—the specific point in time you need your money, say, for a down payment in seven years.

The Walk Itself (The Holding Period Return): This is the total, real-world return you experience on your journey. It's the sum of the melody (coupons), the echoes (reinvestment), and the effect of any market winds that might push you up or down (capital gain/loss).

Your Balancing Pole (Macaulay Duration): This is the most crucial tool you have. Macaulay duration isn't the length of the rope (that's maturity); it's the perfectly weighted balancing pole for your specific bond. It represents the "center of gravity" of your investment's cash flows, measured in years. A long, heavy pole (high duration) is very sensitive to the slightest breeze (interest rate changes), while a short, light pole (low duration) is more stable.

The Magic of Immunization: Finding Perfect Balance

Here is where the art of financial tightrope walking comes alive. The "wind" in this analogy is interest rate risk, and it comes from two directions at once.

Price Risk: A gust of wind from your left (rising interest rates) tries to push you down, causing the value of your balancing pole (your bond's price) to fall.

Reinvestment Risk: A gust of wind from your right (falling interest rates) means the energy you get from stepping forward (reinvesting coupons) is weaker, slowing your momentum.

The magic happens when you choose a balancing pole (Macaulay duration) that is the exact length of your walk (investment horizon).

If interest rates rise (a gust from the left), the value of your pole drops (capital loss). But this same gust allows you to take stronger, more powerful steps forward as you reinvest your coupons at higher rates. The extra reinvestment income perfectly cushions your fall. You stay on the rope.

If interest rates fall (a gust from the right), your steps become weaker as you reinvest coupons at lower rates. But this same gust lifts your pole, increasing its value (capital gain). The lift from the pole's increased value perfectly compensates for your weaker steps. You stay on the rope.

When your investment horizon matches the Macaulay duration, you are immunized. The two opposing forces of interest rate risk—price risk and reinvestment risk—cancel each other out. You can walk your financial tightrope with serene confidence, knowing that no matter which way the wind blows, you are perfectly balanced to arrive at your destination with your expected return intact.

If your walk is shorter than your pole (horizon < duration), you're more vulnerable to the wind pushing the pole down (price risk). If your walk is longer than your pole (horizon > duration), you're more vulnerable to your steps becoming weaker (reinvestment risk).

Macaulay Duration: Finding Your Bond's Center of Gravity

So, what exactly is this magical balancing pole? How do we measure it?

Macaulay duration is the weighted-average time until you receive all your money back. It's the "financial center of gravity" for your bond. A zero-coupon bond that only pays you at maturity has its center of gravity at the very end—its duration equals its maturity. But a bond that pays coupons along the way has its center of gravity pulled closer to the present, so its duration is always less than its maturity.

Calculating Your Balancing Pole

Finding this center of gravity is a beautiful exercise in seeing the value of money through time.

Map the Future: First, you lay out every single cash flow you will ever receive from the bond—each coupon and the final principal.

Pull It All to Today: Money in the future is worth less than money today. Using the bond's yield to maturity (YTM) as our "time machine," we discount each of those future payments to find its present value (PV).

$PV=(1+YTM)tCF$

Where CF is the cash flow, YTM is the yield per period, and t is the time period.

Find Each Payment's "Weight": The bond's price is the sum of all these present values. To find the importance, or "weight," of each cash flow, you divide its present value by the total price of the bond.

Weightt=Bond PricePVt

Find the Balance Point: Now, you simply multiply each cash flow's weight by the time period (t) in which it arrives. Summing all these up gives you the final number—the Macaulay duration. It's the single point in time where the present values of all cash flows on either side are perfectly balanced.

Macaulay Duration=Σ (Weightt×t)

What the Number Really Means

Once you have your Macaulay duration, you hold a powerful insight:

A Measure of Sensitivity: It's the most intuitive gauge of interest rate risk. A bond with a duration of 7 years will move (inversely) about 7% in price for every 1% change in interest rates. The longer the duration, the more dramatic the price swing.

Your Immunization Target: As we saw, it's the precise target for your investment horizon if you wish to neutralize interest rate risk.

A True Comparison Tool: It allows you to compare the real risk of vastly different bonds. A 20-year bond with high coupons might actually have a shorter duration—and be less risky—than a 10-year bond with zero coupons.

By understanding Macaulay duration, you move from being a passive listener to an active conductor of your financial future. You're no longer just holding a bond; you're holding a finely tuned instrument, and now you know exactly how to play it.

Yield-Based Bond Duration Measures and Properties

Your Bond is a Seesaw ⚖️

Think of your bond as sitting on one end of a seesaw. On the other end, pulling it up or down, is the world of interest rates. When interest rates go up, your bond's price goes down. When rates fall, your bond's price rises. It's a simple, inverse relationship.

But not all seesaws are built the same. Some are long and incredibly wobbly, while others are short and stable. Understanding your bond's specific seesaw—how it moves and why—is the key to mastering interest rate risk. Three special tools help us measure this wobble: Modified Duration, Money Duration, and PVBP.

Measuring the Wobble: From a Tilt to a Price Tag

Let's break down how we measure the sensitivity of your bond's seesaw.

Modified Duration: How Steep is the Tilt?

Modified duration tells you how sensitive your seesaw is. It answers the question: "If interest rates take one big step up (a 1% change), what percentage will my bond's price drop?"

Imagine a bond with a modified duration of 5. This means for every 1% jump in prevailing interest rates, your bond's price is expected to fall by about 5%. If rates fall by 1%, your bond's price will jump up by 5%. A higher duration means you're on a longer, more dramatic seesaw—more risk, but also more potential reward from favorable rate moves.

Money Duration & PVBP: Putting a Dollar Value on the Move 💰

Percentage tilts are useful, but what we really care about is money. That's where these next two concepts come in.

Money Duration (or Dollar Duration) translates that percentage tilt into cold, hard cash. It tells you the actual dollar amount your bond's price will change for that 1% shift in interest rates.

How it works: Simply take the percentage change (modified duration) and apply it to your bond's price. If our bond with a duration of 5 is worth $1,000, its money duration is $50 ($1,000 x 5%). So, a 1% rate hike would cause the bond's value to drop by about $50.

Price Value of a Basis Point (PVBP) is for the detail-oriented. 🔬 It measures the dollar impact of the smallest possible move: a tiny, one-basis-point (0.01%) nudge in interest rates.

How it works: Since we know the dollar change for a 100-basis-point move is $50 (from our money duration), we just divide that by 100.

PVBP=100$50=$0.50

This means for every tiny 0.01% uptick in rates, your bond's price will dip by just 50 cents. It's the perfect tool for traders who need to see the financial impact of every little market tremor.

What Makes Your Seesaw Wobble? The 3 Key Factors

So, why are some bond-seesaws long and volatile while others are short and sturdy? It comes down to three main characteristics.

1. Maturity: The Longer the Board, the Bigger the Swing

This is the most straightforward rule. The longer a bond's maturity, the higher its duration and the riskier it is.

Think about it. A 30-year bond is a very long seesaw plank. A small push on the "interest rate" end sends the "price" end flying way up or down. You have to wait 30 years to get your principal back, leaving you exposed to three decades of potential rate changes. A 2-year bond, on the other hand, is a short, stubby plank. It's much more stable because you get your money back soon, making it less vulnerable to long-term rate shenanigans.

2. Coupon Rate: The Helper in the Middle

A bond's coupon rate acts like a stabilizing force. The higher the coupon rate, the lower the duration and the less risky the bond.

Imagine a high-coupon bond as having a helpful friend sitting near the center of the seesaw. The weight of their regular, heavy payments (the coupons) helps anchor the board, making it less sensitive to what's happening at the other end. You're getting more of your money back sooner, which reduces your overall risk. A zero-coupon bond is the opposite—it's just you on one end and interest rates on the other, with no helper in the middle. It's the wobbliest of all.

3. Yield Level: The Starting Position of the Seesaw

This one is a bit counter-intuitive. The higher a bond's starting yield, the lower its duration and interest rate risk.

Picture the seesaw's starting position.

Low-Yield World: When yields are extremely low (e.g., 1%), the "interest rate" end of the seesaw is already way up in the air. It's in a precarious, sensitive position. Even a small downward nudge (a rate increase) will cause a large, dramatic swing on your "price" end.

High-Yield World: When yields are high (e.g., 8%), the "interest rate" end is already close to the ground. Pushing it down further has much less of a dramatic effect; it simply doesn't have as far to fall. The price has already been "discounted" by the high yield, making it less sensitive to further changes.

By seeing your bond as a seesaw, you can intuitively grasp how maturity, coupons, and yield create its unique risk profile. This simple shift in perspective turns abstract financial metrics into a tangible story of balance, leverage, and risk.

Yield-Based Bond Convexity and Portfolio Properties

1. Beyond the Straight and Narrow: Understanding a Bond's Smile

Let's talk about one of the most elegant concepts in fixed income: convexity. It's the secret sauce that separates a good bond from a great one, especially when interest rates start acting wild.

What is This "Convexity" You Speak Of?

Imagine you're driving down a long, straight road. Your speedometer tells you your speed right now. That's duration. It gives you a great, simple estimate of how much your bond's price will change if interest rates just nudge a little. For a tiny tap on the brakes, the speedometer is all you need.

But what if you're heading for a sharp turn? Your speedometer alone won't tell the whole story. You need to understand how your car handles the curve. That's convexity.

In the world of bonds, the relationship between a bond's price and its yield isn't a straight line—it's a curve. Convexity is the measure of that curve. For most bonds, this curve is a gift. It looks like a slight, gentle smile.

This "smile" of positive convexity is your best friend as an investor:

When interest rates fall, your bond's price doesn't just go up; it goes up at an accelerating rate. You're riding the steepening part of the smile upwards. More gain for your pain.

When interest rates rise, your bond's price doesn't just fall; it falls at a decelerating rate. The smile flattens out, cushioning the blow. Less pain for no gain.

It's a classic "heads you win more, tails you lose less" scenario, a built-in shock absorber that makes the ride through volatile markets a whole lot smoother.

The Engine Under the Hood: The Calculation

So, how do we measure this magical curve? While the math looks intimidating, the idea behind it is quite poetic. The formula essentially gives more importance to cash flows that are further in the future, because those distant payments are the ones that contribute most to the bond's curvature.

For the quants among us, the approximate modified convexity (C) is calculated like this:
$C=P\times(1+y)21t=1\ \Sigma T(1+y)tCFt\times t\times(t+1)$

Where:

P = The bond's price

CF_t = The cash you get at time t

y = The bond's yield-to-maturity (as a decimal)

t = The time period for each cash flow

T = The grand finale, the last period until maturity

Don't let the symbols scare you. Just remember what it's doing: measuring the smile. A bigger number means a bigger, more protective smile.

2. Putting It to the Test: From Theory to Your Wallet

Knowing the theory is great, but let's see how convexity actually saves you money. We can estimate a bond's price change by combining the blunt force of duration with the finesse of convexity.

The formula is a two-part story:
Percentage Price Change≈The Initial Hit(−MD×Δy)+The Convexity Cushion(21×C×(Δy)2)

The first part is the Duration Effect. It's the straightforward, linear estimate.

The second part is the Convexity Adjustment. This is the magic. Notice that the change in yield (Δy) is squared, so this term is always positive for a bond with positive convexity, whether rates go up or down. It's always working in your favor.

Let's Take a Test Drive:

Imagine you own a bond with these specs:

Modified Duration (MD) = 7.5 years

Convexity (C) = 60

The market whispers that yields are about to jump by 0.50% (which is 0.005).

Let's brace for impact.

The Initial Hit (Duration Effect):
$-MD \times \Delta y = -7.5 \times 0.005 = -0.0375 or -3.75\%$

Ouch. Based on duration alone, we're expecting a 3.75% price drop.

The Convexity Cushion (The Adjustment):
$21 \times C \times (\Delta y) 2 = 21$
$\times 60 \times (0.005) 2 = 30 \times 0.000025 = 0.00075 or +0.075\%$

There it is. A small but mighty positive boost. Convexity is pushing back against the loss.

The Final Tally (Total Price Change):
$Total\ Change \approx -3.75\% + 0.075\% = -3.675\%$

So, instead of losing 3.75%, your bond's price is only expected to fall by 3.675%. That little 0.075% difference is convexity earning its keep. It might not seem like much here, but in a multi-million dollar portfolio facing a major rate shock, this "cushion" can translate into saving thousands or even millions of dollars.

3. The Big Picture: A Portfolio's Personality and Its Blind Spots

You don't just own one bond; you own a portfolio—a team. You can calculate the duration and convexity for your entire team to understand its overall character.

Calculating Your Team's Stats

It's refreshingly simple. The duration or convexity of your portfolio is just the weighted average of the individual bonds inside it.

Portfolio Duration = $(w1 \times MD1)+(w2 \times MD2)+\ldots$

Portfolio Convexity = $(w1 \times C1)+(w2 \times C2)+\ldots$

Here, w is the weight of each bond (its market value as a slice of your total portfolio pie), and MD and C are its individual stats. This gives you a powerful top-down view of your portfolio's sensitivity to interest rate swings.

A Word of Caution: The Limits of the Map

As powerful as these tools are, they are like a map of the terrain, not the terrain itself. It's crucial to know their limitations.

The "Perfect World" Problem: These calculations assume the entire yield curve moves in perfect, parallel harmony. Reality is messier. The curve can twist, steepen, or flatten, with short-term rates doing a tango while long-term rates waltz. This "non-parallel shift" can throw off our neat predictions.

Bonds with Trapdoors: The formulas work best for plain-vanilla bonds. Bonds with embedded options—like callable bonds that the issuer can snatch back early, or putable bonds you can sell back to them—are financial chameleons. Their duration and convexity can change dramatically as rates move, and our simple formulas can be fooled. For these, you need more advanced tools like "effective duration" and "effective convexity."

Ignoring the Uninvited Guest: Duration and convexity are obsessed with one thing: interest rate risk. They are completely blind to credit risk. If your bond's issuer gets into financial trouble and its credit rating is downgraded, the price will plummet for reasons that have nothing to do with interest rates.

A Snapshot in a Moving World: Duration and convexity are a photograph, not a movie. They tell you your risk profile right now. But as time marches on and markets churn, these numbers change. Your portfolio's risk profile needs to be continuously monitored and re-evaluated.

In the grand symphony of fixed income, duration is the rhythm and convexity is the soul. Understanding duration keeps you in time, but appreciating convexity is what allows you to truly feel the music. By mastering both their power and their limitations, you can navigate the bond market not just with precision, but with wisdom.

Curve-Based and Empirical Fixed-Income Risk Measures

1. The Bond's Hidden Story: Why "Effective" Duration and Convexity Matter

Imagine you buy a concert ticket for a show a year from now. The date, time, and seat are printed right on it. That's a "plain vanilla" bond—its payments (the "show") are fixed and predictable. You can use simple tools to figure out how valuable that ticket is if, say, a competing festival is announced.

But now, imagine your concert ticket has some fine print. It says the band can cancel and refund your money if they get a better offer to play a stadium tour (a callable bond). Or maybe it says you can get a refund if another legendary band you love more announces a show on the same night (a putable bond).

Suddenly, the "show" isn't guaranteed. Its future depends on other events—in the bond world, those events are changes in interest rates. The predictable train schedule of payments has been replaced with a set of possibilities.

This is where the standard rulebook gets tossed out, and we need smarter tools.

Effective Duration: The Street-Smart Sensitivity Gauge

Traditional duration measures are like reading the original, printed schedule. They assume the train will run exactly as planned. But that's not the world of bonds with options.

Effective duration is the "what-if" analysis. It doesn't just look at the bond's blueprint; it asks questions. What if interest rates plummet? The issuer of your callable bond will likely "call" it back, like the band cancelling your show for that stadium tour. They'll pay you back early so they can borrow new money more cheaply. This puts a lid on how much your bond's price can rise. You thought you'd be getting richer as rates fell, but the issuer pulls the plug.

Effective duration captures this real-world behavior. It runs simulations of different interest rate futures to see how the bond's price actually changes when the likelihood of these options being used shifts. It's not a theoretical guess; it's a street-smart measure of how your bond will likely react in the wild, accounting for all the fine print.

Effective Convexity: Reading the Bond's Mood

Duration is a great first guess, but it sees the world in straight lines. It predicts that for every 1% rates go down, the price goes up by a set amount. But the relationship between a bond's price and interest rates is curved, not straight. This curve is its "convexity."

For bonds with options, this curve can get weird. Think about that callable bond again. As interest rates fall, its price goes up, but only to a point. As it gets closer to the price at which the issuer can call it back (the "call price"), the bond's price rally slows down and eventually flat-lines. It knows it has a ceiling.

This creates negative convexity. The price-yield curve, which should be bending favorably toward you, starts bending away. It's like your bond is getting excited about falling rates, then suddenly remembers its leash and gets gloomy.

Effective convexity measures this complex mood. It's a second-level insight that tells you how the bond's duration itself changes as rates move. It accounts for the "bend," the "ceiling," and the "leash" imposed by the embedded option, giving you a far more accurate picture of what to expect, especially when interest rates make big moves.

In short, for bonds with hidden plot twists, effective duration and convexity are the tools that let you read the whole story, not just the cover.

2. The Investor's Crystal Ball: Predicting Price Changes

So, you have these two powerful readings—effective duration and effective convexity. How do you use them to look into the future? You use a formula that acts as a surprisingly accurate crystal ball for your bond's price.

Think of it like predicting a car's journey.

Estimated % Price Change $\approx$ (The Main Engine) + (The Fine-Tuning)

Let's translate that into finance-speak:
$\%\Delta P \approx -(\text{Effective Duration} \times \Delta Y) + (21 \times \text{Effective Convexity} \times (\Delta Y)2)$

Let's pop the hood on this formula:

The Main Engine: - (Effective Duration × ΔY)
This is your first, best guess. Duration tells you the raw power of the price move. The negative sign is crucial—it's the seesaw effect. When yields (ΔY) go up, prices (P) go down, and vice versa. This part of the formula does the heavy lifting.

The Fine-Tuning: + (½ × Effective Convexity × $(\Delta Y)^2$)
This is the convexity adjustment, and it's the secret sauce. It accounts for the curve in the road. Duration

assumes the road is a perfectly straight line, but convexity knows there are bends. This term refines the engine's raw estimate, making it much more accurate, especially for big turns (large yield changes). Notice the yield change (ΔY) is squared, meaning this adjustment becomes much more influential the bigger the rate change.

Let's Take It for a Spin

Imagine your bond has an Effective Duration of 7.5 and an Effective Convexity of 50.
The benchmark yield is 3.00%. What happens if it moves by 50 basis points (which is 0.50%, or 0.0050 as a decimal)?

Scenario A: The Unfriendly Skies (Yields Rise by 0.50%)

Here, $\Delta Y = +0.0050$.

Main Engine: $-(7.5 \times 0.0050) = -0.0375$ (a 3.75% drop)

Fine-Tuning: $+ (0.5 \times 50 \times (0.0050)^2) = +0.000625$ (a tiny positive nudge)

Total Change $\approx -0.0375 + 0.000625 = -0.036875$

The crystal ball says your bond's price will fall by about 3.69%. The convexity adjustment softened the blow, just a little.

Scenario B: The Tailwind (Yields Fall by 0.50%)

Here, $\Delta Y = -0.0050$.

Main Engine: $-(7.5 \times -0.0050) = +0.0375$ (a 3.75% gain)

Fine-Tuning: $+ (0.5 \times 50 \times (-0.0050)^2) = +0.000625$ (another tiny positive nudge)

Total Change $\approx$ +0.0375 + 0.000625 = +0.038125

The crystal ball says your bond's price will rise by about 3.81%. This time, the convexity adjustment gave your returns an extra boost.

See how the price gain (3.81%) was bigger than the price loss (3.69%)? That's the magic of positive convexity at work. It's a feature that makes your bond a smarter, more resilient traveler in the volatile world of interest rates.

3. Beyond the Sway: Key Rate Duration and the Shape of Risk

Thinking that all interest rates move together in perfect harmony—a "parallel shift"—is like assuming an entire suspension bridge only ever sways uniformly side-to-side. In reality, the wind can create complex forces. The middle might twist, one end might dip, or the whole structure might ripple.

The yield curve behaves the same way. Sometimes short-term rates soar while long-term rates barely budge (a flattening). Other times, the opposite happens (a steepening). This is called shaping risk, and it can catch investors off guard if they only look at one number for duration.

Enter Key Rate Duration: The Structural Engineer's Toolkit

Key rate duration is the financial equivalent of a structural engineer tapping different points on the bridge to see how each individual section vibrates. Instead of one number, it gives you a set of durations, each one tied to a specific "key rate" maturity on the yield curve (e.g., the 2-year rate, the 5-year, the 10-year, etc.).

It answers the question: "If the 5-year interest rate moves by a tiny amount, and nothing else changes, how much will my bond's price move?"

Why This Is a Game-Changer:

X-Ray Vision: It provides a granular, X-ray view of your portfolio's sensitivity. You might find that your bond portfolio has a modest overall duration but is terrifyingly sensitive to a change in the 10-year rate. You've just discovered a hidden vulnerability.

Mastering the "Twist": Portfolio managers use key rate durations to protect against, or even profit from, changes in the yield curve's shape. If you expect the curve to flatten, you can use key rate durations to find bonds that will benefit from that specific scenario and adjust your holdings accordingly.

Smarter Hedging: It allows for precision hedging. Instead of using one broad instrument to hedge all interest rate risk, you can use specific instruments to hedge the risk at the most vulnerable points of the curve.

A Reality Check: As a bonus, if you add up all the individual key rate durations for a bond, they should equal its overall effective duration. It's a beautiful way to see how the total risk is distributed across the different maturities.

Effective duration tells you if the bridge will sway. Key rate duration tells you where it's most likely to bend or break. In today's markets, knowing the difference is everything.

4. The Lab vs. The Field: Analytical vs. Empirical Duration

When we try to measure a bond's interest rate risk, we can take two very different approaches. It's like the difference between a lab scientist working from a blueprint and a field biologist observing an animal in the wild.

Analytical Duration: The Lab Scientist's Blueprint

Analytical duration is born from mathematical models and theory. Measures like Macaulay, modified, and even the sophisticated effective duration are all analytical. They are the "lab scientists" of the bond world.

How it Works: They take a bond's specifications—its coupon, maturity, call features—and plug them into a precise formula. They work in a controlled, theoretical environment.

The Big Assumption: A key part of this controlled environment is the assumption that a bond's credit spread (the extra yield it pays over a super-safe government bond) stays constant. The model isolates the effect of benchmark interest rate changes, assuming nothing else interferes.

The Result: You get a clean, forward-looking prediction based on how the bond should behave according to financial theory. It's the blueprint.

Empirical Duration: The Field Biologist's Notebook

Empirical duration doesn't start with a formula; it starts with a question: "What actually happened?" It's the "field biologist" who watches the bond in its natural habitat—the market.

How it Works: It uses statistical analysis (like regression) on historical data. It looks back at months or years of the bond's price movements and compares them to the movements of benchmark interest rates.

The Big Difference: It captures the messy, real-world chaos. Crucially, it sees how credit spreads actually behave. During a "flight to quality" crisis, for example, government bond yields may fall, but the fear of default can make corporate credit spreads widen dramatically. The field biologist sees that when the storm comes, the animal (the corporate bond) doesn't just react to the rain (benchmark rates); it also reacts to the predators (credit fears).

The Result: You get a duration measure that reflects how the bond has actually behaved, with all the complex interactions included. It's the notebook full of real-world observations.

Feature	Analytical Duration (The Lab Scientist)	Empirical Duration (The Field Biologist)
Source	Mathematical formulas, bond blueprints	Historical market data, observation
Credit Spreads	Assumes they are constant (a controlled variable)	Captures their actual historical movement
Best For...	Government Bonds: In a sterile environment with no predators (credit risk), the blueprint is very accurate.	Corporate Bonds: In a complex ecosystem, observing real behavior is key, especially during market stress.
Perspective	How a bond should behave in theory.	How a bond has behaved in reality.

So, which is better? Neither. They are two different lenses for viewing the same risk. The lab scientist gives you the fundamental mechanics, while the field biologist tells you the survival story. A truly wise investor uses the insights from both the lab and the field to navigate the complex world of fixed income.

Credit Risk

1. The Ghost in the Machine: Getting to the Heart of Credit Risk

Every loan, every bond, every extension of credit is built on a simple, ancient promise: "I will pay you back." But shadowing that promise is a quiet, persistent question: "...But what if they don't?" That question, that uncertainty, is the ghost in the financial machine. We call it credit risk. It's the raw, unnerving possibility that a borrower's promise will shatter, leaving the lender with empty hands and a hole in their balance sheet.

To understand this ghost, we must know its two distinct forms: the chance it will appear, and the damage it will do when it does.

First, there's the Probability of Default (PD), which is the financial world's attempt to predict the future. Think of it as a weather forecast for a borrower's ability to pay. A 2% PD is like a meteorologist telling you there's a 2% chance of a thunderstorm next year. It's not a guarantee of sunshine, but it's reassuring. This forecast is pieced together from clues: the borrower's financial health (are they thriving or barely surviving?), the economic climate (is it a boom time or a downturn?), and their personal history (are they a reliable friend or a flake?). A stormy forecast—a high PD—makes any lender nervous, and they'll demand a higher price (interest rate) to venture out into that potential rain.

But what happens if the storm hits? That's where Loss Given Default (LGD) comes in. This isn't about if the borrower defaults, but about how bad the damage is when they do. A default doesn't always mean a total loss. Imagine you loaned a friend $100,000 to buy a car. If they default, you don't lose the full amount, because you can still seize and sell the car. If you get $40,000 back from the sale, your true loss is $60,000, making your LGD 60%. LGD is all about the "life raft." Does the loan have collateral, like property or equipment, that can be salvaged from the wreckage? Is your claim at the front of the line (senior debt) or the back (subordinated debt)? A well-secured loan with a strong legal claim is like having a sturdy life raft and a flare gun, dramatically lowering the potential loss even if the ship goes down.

2. The Gatekeepers of Trust: The Power and Peril of Credit Ratings

In the vast, anonymous ocean of global finance, how does anyone know who to trust? Enter the Credit Rating Agencies (CRAs). These are the official storytellers of the financial world. They issue what are essentially financial report cards—or, perhaps more accurately, judgments—on the trustworthiness of companies and even entire countries. Their famous letter grades, from the gilded "AAA" to the ominous "C," are intended to be a universal language of risk.

Their power is immense. For investors, a high rating is a green light, a seal of approval that signals a safe harbor for their capital. It's a shortcut through the dense fog of financial data, especially for huge funds that are mandated to only invest in highly-rated securities. For the companies being rated, a strong grade is a golden key. It unlocks the door to cheaper borrowing, saving them millions and fueling their growth. In this way, ratings act as a crucial lubricant, making the gears of global capital turn more smoothly and transparently.

But these storytellers are not infallible gods; they are fallible mortals, and their stories have limitations. First, their ratings are opinions, not prophecies. They are educated guesses based on models and historical data, but they can be wrong, sometimes spectacularly so. Second, they are often looking in the rearview mirror. A rating might reflect a company's glorious past right up until the moment it drives off a cliff. There's a lag, and in finance, timing is everything.

The most potent criticism, however, is the inherent conflict of interest. The companies being rated are the ones who pay the agencies for the rating. This "issuer-pays" model raises the uncomfortable question: can a storyteller be truly objective when the subject of the story is also their client? It's like a restaurant critic being paid by the chef. Furthermore, the immense power of these ratings can create a "cliff effect." A single downgrade can trigger a panic, a digital stampede of sellers that can push a struggling company into a death spiral. It's a reminder that while these ratings are a useful guide, relying on them blindly is like outsourcing your own judgment—a risky move in any part of life.

3. The Price of Worry: Decoding the Whispers of Yield Spreads

Why would an investor buy a risky corporate bond when they could own an ultra-safe U.S. Treasury bond? For one reason: they get paid more to do it. That "extra pay" is the yield spread. Think of it as the "price of worry"—the compensation an investor demands for taking on the risk of lending to a less-than-perfect borrower. This spread isn't static; it breathes, widening and shrinking in response to three powerful forces.

First is the Economic Weather. When the sun is shining and the economy is booming, companies are healthy, defaults are rare, and worry is cheap. Yield spreads shrink. But when a recession looms like a gathering storm, fear creeps in, the perceived risk of default rises, and investors demand a much higher price for their worry, causing spreads to widen dramatically. Other atmospheric conditions matter, too. High inflation is like a slow leak in a tire, eroding future returns, so investors demand higher yields to keep moving. A central bank raising interest rates is like changing the gravitational pull of the entire system, shifting all risk calculations.

Next is the Mood of the Market. This is about the psychology of the crowd. Is the market feeling brave and optimistic (a "risk-on" environment), snapping up risky assets and shrinking spreads? Or is it terrified and pessimistic (a "risk-off" environment), stampeding toward the safety of government bonds and causing spreads on everything else to blow out? This mood is also swayed by liquidity—how easily you can sell a bond. A bond that's hard to sell is like being in a crowded theater with only one exit; you'd demand a better seat (a higher yield) for that anxiety. A massive new supply of bonds can also flood the market, temporarily forcing sellers to offer better prices (wider spreads) to attract buyers.

Finally, we zoom in on the Character of the Company. This is the most personal and direct driver of a bond's spread. What is the borrower's financial DNA? A company with a fortress-like balance sheet and steady profits will have a razor-thin spread. A highly indebted company in a volatile industry will have to pay a hefty premium. This is where credit ratings play their part, offering a quick summary of the company's character. But it goes deeper. The very structure of the bond matters. Are you at the front of the line to get paid in a bankruptcy (senior debt), or at the back (subordinated debt)? Your place in the rescue line determines your risk and your reward. The bond's covenants—the rules of the game designed to protect investors—can also act as a safety net, giving investors the confidence to accept a tighter spread.

Credit Analysis for Government Issuers

Reading the Soul of a Nation: Sovereign Debt

Lending to a country is the ultimate high-stakes relationship. You can't repossess a nation's capital or liquidate its mountains and rivers if things go south. There's no bankruptcy court for a kingdom. This changes everything. The entire bet rests on two profoundly human concepts: a country's character and its health.

The Character: A Nation's Willingness to Pay

This is the political heartbeat of the deal. A country can be sitting on mountains of gold and still choose to walk away from its debts. Why? Because politics is a messy, passionate business. Imagine a nation's government as its mind and will.

The Public Mood: Is the population simmering with discontent? Are there protests in the streets? A government facing a revolution might find it easier to default on foreign loans than to impose austerity on its angry citizens. The political cost of paying becomes too high.

The Change of Guard: A new regime, swept into power on a wave of populism, might declare the debts of the "corrupt old guard" illegitimate. Suddenly, the promises made yesterday are worth less than the paper they were written on.

The Global Chessboard: A country is never just itself; it's a player in a global drama. Geopolitical winds can blow a nation's intentions off course. Sanctions can choke its financial arteries. A powerful ally might pressure it to honor its debts, while a new rival might encourage it to default. Willingness isn't a fixed trait; it's a fluid state, swayed by the whispers in the halls of power and the roars of the global arena.

The Health: A Nation's Ability to Pay

This is the national physical. It's where we listen to the country's economic pulse and check its vital signs.

The Economic Engine: Is the country's economy a vibrant, humming machine, creating jobs, wealth, and a steady stream of tax revenue? Or is it a sputtering, rusted engine, leaking fuel and grinding to a halt? A nation's GDP growth is its lifeblood.

The Fiscal Diet: We look at the national budget like a household's. Is it living within its means, or is it on a reckless credit card binge, racking up deficits year after year? A skyrocketing debt-to-GDP ratio is a flashing red light, a sign of a body carrying too much weight for its frame.

The Immune System: How does the country handle external shocks? A nation addicted to a single export, like oil, is like a person with a severe allergy—a sudden price drop can trigger a systemic crisis. The country's foreign exchange reserves are its emergency adrenaline shot, a buffer to pay foreign bills when times get tough. Dwindling reserves signal a weakened immune system, vulnerable to the slightest infection from the global economy.

The Internal Chemistry: We even look at the social fabric. Deep-seated inequality or chronic unemployment creates internal stress, a slow-burning fever that can destabilize the entire system. An aging population can be a long-term strain on the nation's financial health, with pensions and healthcare costs stretching its resources to the limit.

The Family Tree of Finance: Non-Sovereign Debt

Now, let's step down from the nation-state to its family members: the cities, provinces, and public utilities. Here, the analysis gets even more personal, focusing on relationships and local dynamics.

The first question is always: Who's got your back? The relationship with the central government is everything. Is this city a favored child, with a powerful parent (the national government) ready to bail it out with an explicit guarantee? Or is it a distant cousin, left to fend for itself? This "intergovernmental support" can be a powerful safety net, but you have to know how strong and reliable its threads are.

Next, we look at their allowance and chores. Unlike a nation that can tax everything, a municipality has a smaller toolkit—property taxes, maybe a local sales tax, or fees from the water utility. How stable are these income streams? Are they growing, or is the local economic base eroding? At the same time, what are its mandated chores? Is the central government forcing it to pay for expensive new schools or healthcare programs without providing the funds? These "unfunded mandates" are the financial equivalent of being given all the responsibility with none of the resources.

Finally, we examine their local governance. Is the city hall run with transparency and competence, or is it a black box of cronyism? Strong, clear-eyed leadership can make a small city a better credit risk than a poorly managed province.

In the end, evaluating government debt isn't for the faint of heart. It's where the cold, hard math of a spreadsheet meets the unpredictable, passionate story of a people. You must be both an analyst and an anthropologist, a historian and a futurist, trying to understand the financial destiny written in a nation's laws, its ledgers, and its soul.

Credit Analysis for Corporate Issuers

The Art and Science of Trust: Peering into a Company's Soul

Before anyone lends a dime, they are trying to answer a single, profound question: "Can I trust you to pay me back?" Answering this isn't about plugging numbers into a cold formula. It's a full-blown investigation, a financial health check-up that combines the intuition of a seasoned detective with the hard data of a forensic scientist. It's about understanding the complete story of a company—not just its bank account, but its very character.

The Story Behind the Numbers: The Qualitative Hunch

This is the art. It's reading the room, looking the leadership in the eye, and understanding the world a company lives in. It's the story that numbers alone can never tell.

The Captains of the Ship (Management & Strategy): You can have the most advanced vessel in the world, but with a reckless or indecisive captain, it's bound for the rocks. Is the leadership team a group of visionary explorers with a map to the future, or are they just reacting to the waves? We look for a seasoned crew with a history of navigating treacherous waters. We want to see their strategic blueprints, listen to how they talk about their challenges, and know there's a succession plan—a first mate ready to take the helm if the captain falls ill.

The Sea Itself (Industry & Competition): Is the company sailing on a calm, predictable lake or weathering a perpetual storm in the North Atlantic? An industry with high barriers to entry is like a protected harbor, safe from pirates (new competitors). A cyclical industry, however, is a wild ocean of booms and busts. We need to know: Is this company the biggest ship in a tiny pond or a tiny ship in a vast, competitive ocean? Does it have a unique flag—a brand, a patent, a secret recipe—that makes everyone want to trade with it, or is it just another boat in the fleet?

The Engine Room (Operations & Supply Chain): A company's true power comes from its engine room. Is it a gleaming, efficient machine that hums with productivity, or a clanking, wasteful mess leaking cash? We look at how it builds its products, manages its supplies, and controls its costs. In today's world, we also trace its lifelines—the supply chain. A company relying on a single supplier in a volatile region is one storm away from disaster. A diversified, resilient supply chain is a sign of a vessel built to last.

The Rules of the Water (Legal & ESG): Every sea has its laws. Is the company navigating them with skill, or is it constantly getting tangled in the nets of regulators and lawsuits? Beyond the law, what is the company's character? Environmental, Social, and Governance (ESG) factors are the modern-day mariner's code. A company that pollutes its own waters, mistreats its crew, or has a corrupt leadership structure is not just unethical—it's a bad risk. It's a ship that will eventually be denied port by customers, investors, and talent alike.

The Hard Vitals: The Quantitative Truth

This is the science. It's the ship's log, the sensor readings, the undeniable metrics that measure the health and performance of the vessel. We use financial ratios to take its pulse.

Immediate Health Check (Liquidity Ratios):

Current Ratio: Current Assets/Current Liabilities. Can you pay all your bills for the next year with what you have on hand?

Quick Ratio: (Current Assets–Inventory)/Current Liabilities. If you had to pay your bills tomorrow, could you do it without having a fire sale on your inventory?

Long-Term Endurance (Solvency Ratios):

Debt-to-Equity Ratio: Total Debt/Shareholders' Equity. How much of the ship is owned by the crew (equity) versus the banks (debt)? Too much debt is like taking on too much ballast—it makes the ship sluggish and hard to maneuver.

Interest Coverage Ratio: EBIT/Interest Expense. Does your engine generate enough power (earnings) to easily handle the cost of your loans (interest)? If this number is low, the engine is straining.

Engine Performance (Profitability Ratios):

Net Profit Margin: Net Income/Revenue. For every dollar of treasure you bring aboard, how many cents are left after paying for the entire voyage?

Return on Assets (ROA): Net Income/Average Total Assets. How good are you at using the ship itself—its cannons, its sails, its very wood—to generate profit?

The Lifeblood (Cash Flow Ratios):

Debt Service Coverage Ratio (DSCR): Operating Cash Flow/Total Debt Service. This is the ultimate test. After a long voyage, is the actual cash in your treasure chest enough to make your loan payments? A ratio below 1.0x means you're taking on water.

The Financial Last Will & Testament: Who Gets a Lifeboat in a Shipwreck?

When disaster strikes and a company goes bankrupt, a brutal but orderly hierarchy emerges. Understanding this "pecking order" is crucial because it determines a lender's real risk of losing everything.

The Lifeboat's VIP Section (Secured Debt): Lenders with secured debt are lashed to a specific, valuable piece of the ship—the anchor, the cannons, or even the whole vessel. If the ship sinks, they get to claim their collateral first. They have a reserved seat on the lifeboat.

The General Cabins (Unsecured Debt): These lenders trusted the captain's word alone. They have no claim on any specific asset. They get a spot on the lifeboat only after all the VIPs are seated.

The Priority Ladder in a Sinking:

The Rescue Crew: Lawyers and administrators managing the bankruptcy get paid first.

The Secured Lenders: They get their collateral, or its cash value.

The Crew & The Taxman: Employees owed wages and the government owed taxes get the next claim. They are priority passengers.

The Unsecured Crowd: Bondholders, suppliers, and other general lenders are next. They share whatever is left, which is often pennies on the dollar.

The Subordinated Lenders: These creditors knowingly agreed to be last in line among lenders, often in exchange for a higher interest rate.

The Owners (Equity Holders): The captains and owners of the ship go down with it. In a bankruptcy, their investment is almost always wiped out completely. They only get what's left after everyone—and I mean everyone—has been paid in full.

This hierarchy is why a Senior Secured Bond gets a stellar credit rating, while a Subordinated Unsecured Note from the very same company gets a much lower one. The first is a ticket for a VIP seat on the lifeboat; the second is a prayer that the ship never, ever sinks.

Ultimately, credit assessment is this beautiful dance between story and statistic, between character and cash flow. It's about knowing the captain, inspecting the engine, reading the sea charts, and, just in case, knowing exactly where the lifeboats are.

Fixed-Income Securitization

The Alchemy of Finance: Turning Possibility into Power

Imagine a vast orchard, heavy with ripe, valuable fruit. The owner of this orchard, let's call her a local banker, has a problem. Her fruit—let's say they're thousands of car loans and home mortgages—is undeniably valuable. But it's stuck on the trees. She can only sell one piece of fruit at a time, and it will take decades for all of them to ripen and be paid off. Her wealth is real, but it's frozen, locked away on her balance sheet. She can't use the value of this future harvest to plant new trees or lend to other farmers in the community.

This is where the magic of securitization begins. It's not a dusty financial term; it's a recipe for unlocking potential. It's the art of taking something solid and illiquid and transforming it into a flowing river of capital.

The Financial Kitchen: A Recipe for Liquidity

At its heart, securitization is a grand, cooperative act of financial cooking. Here's how the kitchen works and who the chefs are:

The Orchard Grower (The Originator): This is our banker, the one who cultivated the fruit in the first place by making loans to her community. She gathers a giant basket of these loans—a diverse mix of apples, pears, and plums—to sell in one go.

The Alchemist's Workshop (The Special Purpose Vehicle - SPV): The banker doesn't sell her fruit at the local market. Instead, she sells the entire harvest to a separate, specially-created entity. Think of it as a pristine, independent juice factory built for one purpose only. This factory is walled off from the original orchard. If a blight (bankruptcy) were to ever hit the orchard, the factory and its inventory are completely safe. This "bankruptcy remote" structure is the cornerstone of trust in the whole process.

The Master Chef & Marketer (The Underwriter): The juice factory hires a master chef, typically a savvy investment bank. This chef decides how to process the fruit. Will they create a simple, pure apple juice? Or a complex, layered smoothie? They design the packaging, price the final products, and create a compelling story to tell the world about their new creation. They are the bridge between the factory and the global marketplace.

The Juice Itself (The Securities): The factory takes the thousand individual pieces of fruit and presses them together, blending their collective cash flows into a single, powerful stream. This stream is then bottled into different types of securities.

The Premium Organic Juice: These are the safest bottles, filled first with the purest stream of cash flow. They promise a steady, reliable return.

The Exotic Smoothie Blend: These bottles get filled next. They carry a bit more risk but offer a more exciting, higher-yield flavor.

The High-Energy Shot: This is the last bit, concentrated and potent. It's the riskiest, but for those with an appetite for adventure, it offers the biggest potential reward.

This process of "tranching" is ingenious. It takes one pool of assets and creates a menu of investment options suitable for every palate.

The Global Tasting Room: Who Drinks the Juice?

The Connoisseurs (The Investors): The world is full of thirsty investors. A pension fund, responsible for a million retirement nest eggs, might buy the safe, premium juice for its reliability. A hedge fund, looking for explosive growth, might grab the high-energy shot. Securitization gives them access to investments they could never find before—a taste of the American housing market, the European auto industry, or a university's student loan portfolio, all neatly bottled and ready to serve. It allows them to diversify, spreading their risk instead of betting it all on one thing.

The Guardians of Quality: To ensure no one is sold snake oil, a few key guardians oversee the process.

The Food Critic (Credit Rating Agency): Independent reviewers like Moody's or S&P taste the juice and give it a rating—AAA for the finest vintage, B- for the table wine. This simple grade gives investors a trusted, shorthand guide to quality.

The Orchard Manager (The Servicer): Someone has to keep collecting the monthly payments from the original borrowers—the people who bought the cars and homes. This manager ensures the cash keeps flowing from the roots to the factory.

The Customer Advocate (The Trustee): This is an impartial party, usually a bank, who holds the recipe and legally represents all the investors. They make sure the factory is doing what it promised, ensuring the people who bought the juice get exactly what they paid for.

Why It All Matters: Watering the Economic Garden

When this process works, it's not just the players who win; the entire economy flourishes. The banker who sold her orchard now has a flood of cash. She can plant new trees—meaning she can issue more loans to local businesses, helping a new restaurant open or a tech startup get off the ground.

Capital, once trapped on isolated islands, now flows freely through deep, wide channels, irrigating the entire economic landscape. Risk is no longer concentrated in a few big banks; it's shared across thousands of global investors, making the entire system more resilient and stable. Financial markets become more vibrant, innovative, and efficient—a bustling global bazaar of opportunity.

In essence, securitization is the story of turning static value into dynamic energy. It's a powerful financial tool that, at its best, transforms the quiet potential of a single loan into the roaring engine of a global economy.

Asset-Backed Security (ABS) Instrument and Market Features

1. Covered Bonds: The "Belt and Suspenders" of the Bond World

In the vast universe of investments, covered bonds are the cautious friend who always carries a spare tire, a first-aid kit, and an emergency poncho. What makes them so uniquely secure? It boils down to a simple, powerful promise: dual recourse.

Imagine you're buying a pie from a baker. With most investments (like asset-backed securities), your purchase is a bet on the pie itself. If the pie is delicious, you win. If it's terrible, you've lost your money. That's it.

A covered bond is like buying a pie from a baker who not only promises the pie is good but also says, "If this pie turns out to be anything less than perfect, just come back to me, and I'll give you your money back right out of my own pocket." You have a claim on the pie (the "cover pool" of high-quality loans) and a claim on the baker (the issuing bank). This two-layer safety net is why covered bonds are the gold standard for conservative investors.

The Private Stash (Segregated Cover Pool): The loans backing these bonds aren't just thrown in with the bank's other assets. They're kept in a legally separate, constantly monitored "private stash." The bank must keep this stash overstuffed, a practice called overcollateralization, ensuring there are always more assets in the pool than bonds to be paid.

The Rulebook: This isn't a casual promise; it's enshrined in law. Specific national legislation acts as a rigid rulebook, dictating exactly what can go into the stash and how it must be managed. This transparency builds immense trust.

The primary risk? Even with the best safety nets, if the baker's entire business collapses spectacularly, it could shake your confidence. But short of a total catastrophe, the covered bond's structure makes it one of the most resilient investments you can find.

2. Financial Armor: The Art of Credit Enhancement

How do you turn a pile of everyday loans—car payments, credit card bills—into a fortress-like investment that big-money players want to buy? You build it some armor. This process, called credit enhancement, is all about creating buffers to absorb potential losses. Here's how the financial blacksmiths forge this protection.

Internal Armor (Forged from Within)

The Human Pyramid (Subordination): This is the most classic technique. Imagine a human pyramid. The people on the bottom row (the "junior" or "subordinated" tranches) are bearing the most weight. If someone stumbles, they take the fall first, protecting the people at the very top (the "senior" tranches). Investors in the top tier only get hurt if the entire pyramid collapses.

Packing Extra Snacks (Overcollateralization): You wouldn't go on a long hike with the exact amount of food you think you'll need. You pack extra "just in case." Securitizations do the same. They might bundle $120 million of loans to back just $100 million of securities. That extra $20 million in loans is a delicious cushion against defaults.

The Tip Jar (Excess Spread): Think of the small difference between the interest earned on the loans and the interest paid out to investors. This sliver of profit, or "spread," is collected in a virtual tip jar. If a few loans stop paying, the servicer can dip into the jar to make sure investors don't miss a payment.

The Emergency Fund (Reserve Account): This is like starting your road trip with a full tank of gas and cash in the glove box. A cash reserve is set aside right at the beginning. It sits there, waiting to be used to cover any unexpected bumps in the road, like a sudden spike in delinquencies.

External Armor (Calling for Backup)

The Rich Co-Signer (Surety Bonds & Letters of Credit): Sometimes, the structure needs a powerful ally. A highly-rated insurance company or bank can step in as a co-signer. They issue a guarantee (a surety bond or letter of credit) that says, "If this investment can't pay its bills, we will." This external guarantee makes the investment vastly safer.

3. A Tour of the Financial Zoo: Non-Mortgage Asset-Backed Securities

Step away from the world of mortgages, and you'll find a vibrant zoo of other securitized assets, each with its own unique behavior, diet (cash flows), and dangers (risks).

The Workhorse (Auto Loan-Backed Securities): Backed by car loans, these are the sturdy, reliable Clydesdales of the ABS world. They pull a steady load, delivering predictable monthly payments of principal and interest.

Main Risk: The workhorse stumbles. A borrower might lose their job and default on the loan. During a recession, several horses might stumble at once. Another risk is prepayment—the owner pays off the loan early, and you get your money back sooner than planned, forcing you to find a new place to invest it, possibly at lower rates.

The Hummingbird (Credit Card Receivable-Backed Securities): These are backed by the frenetic, ever-changing balances on our credit cards. Unlike a car loan, there's no finish line. The pool of debt churns constantly as people shop, make payments, and shop again.

Main Risk: The nectar dries up. The value of these securities comes from the high interest rates on revolving balances. If a recession hits and consumers get scared, they might stop spending and start paying off their cards in full. This "yield compression" means less interest is generated, starving the hummingbird of its food source.

The Marathon Runner (Student Loan-Backed Securities): Backed by student debt, this investment is in it for the long haul. The race can last for decades.

Main Risk: Unscheduled rest stops. Student loans come with features like deferment and forbearance, which allow borrowers to pause payments. These "rest stops" can extend the race far longer than anticipated (extension risk), tying up an investor's money. For private loans not backed by the government, the biggest risk is the runner simply dropping out of the race (defaulting).

The Antique Collector (Equipment Lease-Backed Securities): These are backed by leases on big-ticket items like airplanes, railcars, or construction equipment. The cash flow comes from the steady lease payments.

Main Risk: The final auction price. The biggest gamble here is the "residual value." What will that 10-year-old Boeing 737 or combine harvester be worth at the end of its lease? If technology has made it obsolete, its final value could be far lower than projected, leading to a significant loss. It's a bet on the future value of a tangible, aging asset.

4. The Financial Smoothie: Deconstructing Collateralized Debt Obligations (CDOs)

If an ABS is a single-origin coffee, a CDO is a complex, mysterious smoothie. A CDO manager takes hundreds of different "ingredients"—corporate bonds, leveraged loans, even slices of other ABS—and blends them all together in a special purpose vehicle (SPV). They then pour this concoction into different glasses (tranches), each with a distinct flavor and risk profile.

The Senior Glass (AAA-Rated): Poured from the top of the blender, this is the smoothest, purest liquid. It has the least risk and is the first to get paid.

The Mezzanine Glasses (A/BBB-Rated): The middle of the pour. You get more flavor (a higher yield) but also a bit of the pulp and grit. You're taking on more risk and get paid after the senior glass.

The Equity Glass (Unrated): This is the last glass, filled with all the thick, seedy sludge from the bottom of the blender. It absorbs the very first losses if any of the ingredients were spoiled. But if the smoothie is a hit, this glass gets to keep all the leftover profits, making it a high-risk, high-reward gamble.

The Dangers Lurking in the Smoothie

The 2008 financial crisis taught us that these smoothies can be hazardous to your financial health.

Rotten Ingredients (Credit Risk): The smoothie is only as good as what you put in it. If the manager blends in too many low-quality, defaulted loans, the entire concoction will spoil from the bottom up, wiping out the equity and mezzanine glasses.

The Hidden Allergy (Correlation Risk): This was the silent killer of 2008. Managers thought they were diversifying by blending in "different" types of mortgages from California, Florida, and Arizona. But they weren't different fruits; they were all apples from the same orchard—the U.S. housing market. When a single blight (the housing crash) hit the orchard, all the apples went bad at once. The supposed diversification was an illusion.

The Black Box Blender (Structure Risk): The complexity of a CDO can be a feature, but it's also a bug. The structures can be so opaque that investors don't truly know what ingredients are inside or how they interact. You're drinking a smoothie without an ingredient list, trusting that the chef knew what they were doing.

Mortgage-Backed Security (MBS) Instrument and Market Features

1. The Unpredictable Heartbeat: Prepayment Risk and the Art of Time Tranching

Prepayment Risk: The Borrower's Wild Card

Imagine you're an investor who's bought into a stream of mortgage payments. You're counting on that steady, predictable flow of cash, like a reliable river feeding your financial reservoir. But here's the twist: every single homeowner whose loan is in that pool holds a wild card—the right to pay off their loan tomorrow, for any reason at all, with no penalty. This is prepayment risk, the unpredictable heartbeat of the mortgage world.

It's not just a risk; it's a fundamental tension between you and the homeowner. When interest rates fall, homeowners rush to refinance, paying you back in a sudden flood. This isn't a gift. It's contraction risk, and it feels like being handed a wad of cash in the middle of a desert with nothing to buy. You're forced to reinvest your money at the new, disappointingly low rates.

Conversely, when interest rates soar, that prepayment option becomes untouchable. No one wants to refinance. Your investment, which you thought might last seven years, suddenly feels like a life sentence. You're stuck earning a meager 4% while new investments are paying 7%. This is extension risk—the financial equivalent of being stuck in the slow lane while life passes you by. Prepayment risk transforms a simple loan into a complex dance with uncertainty, where the borrower leads, and the investor must follow.

Time Tranching: Conducting the Cash Flow Orchestra

How do you tame this wild river of cash flows? You don't. You become a master hydrologist, building a sophisticated system of dams, canals, and spillways. This is the genius of time tranching. Instead of letting the unpredictable flood of principal and interest payments wash over all investors equally, a securitization carves this flow into different channels, or "tranches," each designed for a different kind of investor.

Sequential Pay Tranches: The First-Class Ticket. Think of a sequential pay structure like boarding a cruise ship. The Tranche A investors are the first-class passengers. When principal payments start flowing, they get paid first, and they get paid all of it until their ticket is punched. They get off the ship early, which is great for those who want a short trip. But they bear the full force of contraction risk—if prepayments come in fast, their trip could be over before it really begins. Meanwhile, the Tranche B and C investors wait patiently on the lower decks. Their journey is much longer, making them vulnerable to extension risk if the ship slows to a crawl. They trade early repayment for a longer, more defined horizon.

Planned Amortization Class (PAC) Tranches: The VIP Lounge. PAC tranches are for investors who despise surprises. They are designed to be an oasis of calm. A PAC tranche is given a "prepayment band"—a high and low speed limit. As long as prepayments stay within this lane, the PAC investor receives a perfectly predictable, scheduled payment. How? It's protected by companion (or support) tranches that act as its bodyguards. If prepayments come in too fast, the bodyguards leap in front and absorb the extra cash. If they come in too slow, the bodyguards sacrifice their own payments to make sure the PAC investor is paid on time. In exchange for this five-star protection, PAC investors typically accept a lower yield. The support tranches, by contrast, live a life of volatility, taking on the risk for a higher potential reward. It's the ultimate trade-off between stability and yield.

Target Amortization Class (TAC) Tranches: TAC tranches are like PACs, but with a one-sided guarantee. They offer protection against prepayments coming in too fast (contraction risk) but leave the investor exposed if payments slow down (extension risk). It's like having a bodyguard who only watches your back from one direction.

2. The DNA of a Securitizable Home Loan

Not just any loan can be bundled up and sold to global investors. The residential mortgages that fuel the securitization engine share a distinct genetic code that makes them perfect for the process.

The Steady Heartbeat (Amortizing): Most U.S. home loans are designed to self-destruct, but in a good way. Each monthly payment is a blend of interest and a bit of principal, a rhythm that slowly but surely pays down the debt. This predictable, amortizing nature is the reliable heartbeat that gives a mortgage-backed security its lifeblood.

The Anchor in the Storm (Secured by Real Estate): This isn't just a financial promise; it's backed by dirt, wood, and brick. The house itself is the collateral. If the borrower defaults, the trust that holds the loan can foreclose on the property. This tangible anchor dramatically reduces the credit risk, giving investors confidence that there's real value behind the paper.

The Long Runway (Maturity Periods): With typical terms of 15 or 30 years, residential mortgages offer a long runway of cash flows. This extended horizon is what gives financial artists the time and space to work their magic, carving out the short, medium, and long-term tranches that appeal to different investors.

The Quality Control Stamp (Standardized Underwriting): To be pooled, especially by government-backed agencies like Fannie Mae and Freddie Mac, loans must be clones of each other in terms of quality. Underwriting standards act as a strict recipe, dictating the required credit scores, loan-to-value (LTV) ratios, and income levels. This standardization ensures that the pool is a consistent, transparent, and trustworthy blend of ingredients.

The Escape Hatch (Prepayment Option): This is the feature that introduces all the drama. The American homeowner's sacred right to prepay their loan at any time is the source of all prepayment risk. It's the ultimate escape hatch for the borrower and the ultimate source of uncertainty for the investor.

The Ground Crew (Servicing): Behind every security is a servicer—the unsung hero who does the groundwork. They collect the monthly checks, manage tax and insurance escrows, chase down late payments, and ensure the cash makes its way from the homeowner's bank account to the investor's portfolio, taking a small fee for keeping the entire machine running smoothly.

Strength in Numbers (Large Pools): Securitization isn't about one loan; it's about thousands. By pooling a vast number of mortgages from different people in different places, the structure diversifies away the idiosyncratic risk of any one person losing their job or any one town facing a downturn.

3. A Tale of Two Securities: RMBS Explained

Residential Mortgage-Backed Securities (RMBS) are the investment products built from this raw material. They come in two main flavors: the simple and direct, and the complex and engineered.

Mortgage Pass-Throughs: The Pane of Glass

The mortgage pass-through is the simplest form of RMBS. Think of it as a clear pane of glass. You look through it and see the underlying pool of mortgages directly.

What it is: The pass-through does exactly what its name implies: it passes all the cash flows (principal and interest) from the mortgage pool directly to investors on a pro-rata basis, minus a small fee for servicing and guarantees. If you own 1% of the security, you get exactly 1% of the net cash that flows from the homeowners.

The Experience: You are completely exposed to the elements. You feel every ripple of prepayment. When homeowners refinance, you get a rush of principal. When they stay put, your cash flow slows to a trickle. There is no structure to shield you.

The Great Divide (Agency vs. Non-Agency): The most critical distinction is whether it's an Agency or Non-Agency pass-through. Agency RMBS are backed by government-sponsored entities (Fannie Mae, Freddie Mac) or a government agency (Ginnie Mae). This backing is a guarantee against default, meaning your credit risk is virtually zero. Non-Agency RMBS, issued by private banks, have no such guarantee. They carry the full risk of homeowner default, and in exchange for that risk, they offer a higher potential yield.

Collateralized Mortgage Obligations (CMOs): The Prism

If a pass-through is a pane of glass, a CMO is a prism. It takes a single, chaotic beam of light—the jumbled cash flows from the mortgage pool—and refracts it into a beautiful, organized spectrum of investable tranches.

What it is: A CMO is a masterwork of financial engineering. It takes the same pool of mortgages that would back a pass-through and uses structures like time tranching to carve it into multiple classes of bonds, each with its own unique risk-and-return profile.

The Experience: The CMO doesn't eliminate prepayment risk; it redistributes it with surgical precision. It allows you to choose your experience. Want stability? Buy the PAC tranche and let the support tranches take the hits for you. Want a short-term investment that pays off quickly? Buy the first sequential tranche. Want to take on more risk for a higher yield? Buy a support tranche or a longer-term sequential bond.

The Trade-off: CMOs offer a tailored, customized solution for investors. This customization, however, comes with complexity. Evaluating a specific CMO tranche requires a deep understanding of its place in the capital structure and how it will behave when the prepayment winds shift.

4. The Skyscraper Cousin: Commercial Mortgage-Backed Securities (CMBS)

If RMBS are built on the foundation of the American Dream, Commercial Mortgage-Backed Securities (CMBS) are built on the foundations of American commerce. They are the bigger, more complex cousins, backed not by family homes, but by the loans on office towers, shopping malls, hotels, and industrial warehouses. They play by a completely different set of rules.

The DNA of a CMBS

A World of Commerce: The collateral isn't a single home; it's a diverse portfolio of income-producing properties. The health of a CMBS depends not on a family's income, but on office occupancy rates, retail sales, and hotel bookings.

The Corporate Veil (Non-Recourse Loans): Unlike most home loans, the loans in a CMBS are typically non-recourse. If the owner of a skyscraper defaults, the lender can take the building, but they can't go after the owner's other assets. The deal is with the property, and the property alone. This makes the quality and income-generating power of the real estate the single most important factor.

The Day of Reckoning (Balloon Payments): Commercial loans don't gently amortize to zero. They often have a 10-year term with payments calculated as if it were a 30-year loan. This means at the end of the 10 years, a massive balloon payment of the remaining principal is due. This creates the primary risk in CMBS: not if they'll pay early, but if they can pay at all when the giant bill comes due.

The Risks of the Commercial World

Prepayment is Tamed, Extension is the Monster: The freewheeling prepayment option of residential loans doesn't exist here. Commercial loans are locked down with "golden handcuffs" in the form of massive prepayment penalties or a complex process called defeasance, where a borrower must replace their loan with a pile of U.S. Treasury bonds that perfectly replicates the future payments. This makes prepayment risk almost negligible. The real beast is extension risk. If a borrower can't make that huge balloon payment—because they can't find a new lender to refinance or the property value has fallen—the loan defaults. This can dramatically extend the life of the CMBS as a "special servicer" steps in to manage the workout, a process that can take years.

Credit Risk is King: The central risk in CMBS is credit risk. Will the tenants of the office building pay their rent? Will the shoppers at the mall keep showing up? Because the loans are non-recourse, a downturn in the commercial real estate market can be devastating. To manage this, CMBS are structured with powerful credit tranching. The structure is a series of shock absorbers: the riskiest "junior" and "equity" tranches at the bottom are designed to absorb the first wave of losses from defaults, protecting the highly-rated "senior" tranches at the top. This isn't a story about timing; it's a story about who survives a default.

About Author

Azhar ul Haque Sario is a bestselling author and data scientist with a remarkable record of achievement. This Cambridge alumnus brings a wealth of knowledge to his work, holding an MBA, ACCA (Knowledge Level - FTMS College Malaysia and London College of Accountancy, London), BBA, and several Google certifications, including specializations in Google Data Analytics, Google Digital Marketing & E-commerce, and Google Project Management.

With ten years of business experience, Azhar combines practical expertise with his impressive academic background to craft insightful books. His prolific writing has resulted in an astounding 2810 published titles, earning him the record for the maximum Kindle editions and paperback books published by an individual author in one year, awarded by Asia Books of Records in 2024.

ORCID: https://orcid.org/0009-0004-8629-830X
Azhar.sario@hotmail.co.uk
https://www.linkedin.com/in/azharulhaquesario/

www.ingramcontent.com/pod-product-compliance
Lightning Source LLC
Chambersburg PA
CBHW031342230926
51848CB00002B/352
9783384669537